MOM & POP HARDWARE

A KANSAS GIRL'S QUIRKY CHILDHOOD AT MY FOLKS' COMPETING STORES

BETH DeCARBO

"A great book with heart!"
—LARRY HATTEBERG, host of *Hatteberg's People*

Flint Hills Publishing

Mom & Pop Hardware – A Kansas Girl's Quirky
Childhood at My Folks' Competing Hardware
Stores
© Beth DeCarbo 2025
All rights reserved.

ᶻ Flint Hills Publishing

Topeka, Kansas
Tucson, Arizona
www.flinthillspublishing.com

Printed in the U.S.A.

Paperback Book: ISBN 978-1-966323-25-9
Hardback Book ISBN: 978-1-966323-26-6
Electronic Book ISBN 978-1-966323-27-3

Library of Congress Control Number: 2025912089

"Bethy, if I've got a biscuit, you've got half."

—Gene Copeland

Dedicated to my parents and to other proud owners of independent hardware stores across America.

B&G Hardware, left, and Copeland Supply, right, on Main Street in McPherson, Kansas.

AUTHOR'S NOTE

I tell people that I grew up working at my parents' two hardware stores. But that's not entirely true. The place where I *grew up*, where I truly became the person I am today, was the parking lot between their two hardware stores.

Starting when I was 10 years old, I worked for both of my parents, whose hardware stores were located side by side on Main Street in McPherson, a small farm town in central Kansas. And on any given day, my job was to run back and forth across the parking lot between them to help out where I was needed. I look back now, and I can see that those trips across the pavement weren't just from one store to another. That parking lot divided two completely different worlds, with my mom and dad acting as sole sovereigns. They were a window into two different ways of doing business, of relating to people, of raising children, and of approaching *life*. Each time I crossed the parking lot, I morphed into the daughter and the employee each of my parents wanted me to be.

I am sharing these memories because I want to describe for the record my quirky childhood that unfolded in the 1970s and early '80s in the tiny town of McPherson, home to roughly 10,000 souls back then. I want to recall a time that at least *seemed* less complicated. Here, the world felt safer. Many folks didn't bother to lock their doors, and the police stayed busy cracking down on jaywalking, joyriding, and cow tipping. And people—even strangers—seemed friendlier. On the sidewalk, you said hello to others as you passed. On the street, you waved to the other driver as you went by.

Behind closed doors, I'm sure that people had their private pains and struggles. Still, I cherish a childhood that was absent of smartphones and social media. There were no 24-hour newscasts spouting vitriol and divisiveness. We relied on intelligent people, not artificial intelligence. Most important, neighbors could disagree—as all humans are wont to do—without hateful name-calling and permanent labels that made you either an "us" or a "them."

There are mixed emotions in telling my story, but by far my memories are warm and good and touch my heart even today. I have changed some of the names and taken liberties with the timeline and other details to give the narrative more clarity. (Since when was one family's story ever straightforward?) In the end, my goal is to honor the legacy of my parents and celebrate the little Kansas town that supported them and nurtured my family.

After reading this account, perhaps you will one day take Exit 60 off I-135 to see McPherson for yourself. The buildings that were once home to B&G Hardware and Copeland Supply are still standing on the 500 block of North Main. But don't bother stopping—only the memories of my parents, Gene and Betty Copeland, remain.

CONTENTS

Contents continued…

Chapter 12
Tipping Point

Chapter 13
Reunions

Chapter 14
The Summer of 1995

References

1.
THE SUMMER OF 1975

If I had a zillion dollars, I would buy a perfume factory. Inside, there would be a long conveyor belt carrying hundreds of bottles. The belt would line up the tops of the tiny bottles under little spigots that would fill them up with the one and only fragrance my factory would make. Its scent—worn by men and women alike—would evoke feelings that occur only in childhood, and only on one day of the year. I would call my fragrance: The Last Day of School.

I would wear my bottle on a chain that hangs around my neck. And whenever I'm having a bad day, I would take out the stopper and breathe deeply. My lungs would fill with the scent of freshly cut grass, city pool chlorine, and burgers on the grill. I would smell the smoke of exploding fireworks and campfires at Kanopolis Lake. Drawing in the air, I would let the feelings of unbounded joy and unlimited potential wash over me. I imagined myself...

"Bethy, come here!" Dad hollered.

...walking out of my classroom for the very last time. In my arms was a paper sack that carried everything that was inside my desk and my art project that was hanging...

"Bethy, COME HERE!" Dad bellowed a second time.

I leaned my push broom on the wall by the coffee pot and ran to Dad. Next to him stood a wheat farmer in sweat-soaked overalls. It was blazing hot outside, and not much better inside my father's hardware store, where the AC was rasping out a steady stream of tepid air.

"Hurry over to next door and get me one 1/4 x 3-inch bolt and bring it back," Dad commanded.

The farmer needed six of the bolts, and Dad only had five in stock. Without that bolt, the man couldn't get his grain out of the ground. And just to spite him, afternoon thunderstorms threatened to shut down cutting for the rest of the day. Shifting his feet, his face pinched, the farmer made it clear that he couldn't afford any delays.

In my mind, the future of one man's wheat crop hinged entirely on me, a 10-year-old kid. My job was to run as fast as I could to B&G Hardware, located right next door on Main Street, and pick up the pivotal bolt. That hardware store—my father's biggest competitor—was owned by my mother.

I crossed the parking lot and opened the door of my mom's hardware store, feeling a rush of brisk air hitting my face. "Raindrops Keep Fallin' on My Head" played softly on KNEX, the local radio station. Mom stood next to a customer, who was quietly studying a 25-foot garden hose like his very life depended on it. At the freight desk, Arlene systematically affixed wee-little price stickers onto individual drill bits.

The antique oak cabinetry, metal bins, and old-fashioned cash register that were in use at B&G Hardware.

6

"Slow down, Bethy," my mom said firmly as I darted to the back of the store to pick up the bolt.

I switched from a trot to a ladylike gait, because according to my mom, it made her hardware store feel "classy." In her mind, the old oak display cases, the glass jars with 10-cent stick candy and the antique tools that hung on the walls gave the place an *olde thyme* feel. Walking at a glacial pace, I passed by faucet gaskets, egg timers, vacuum cleaner bags, brass hinges, and other merchandise on my way to the bins of bolts way in the back of the store. When you're in a hurry, the journey takes roughly two years. Grabbing the bolt, I walked ladylike to the front counter and wrote on a pad: 1/4 x 3 hex bolt, 11¢.

When I got back to the front, Mom was standing next to the same customer, who was still studying the same garden hose. Glancing up, Mom said, "Bethy, can you bring me back a Pepsi?" I mashed the "No Sale" button on her cash register and took out a quarter for her afternoon pop. Then, I tore out across the parking lot, which felt like the front porch of hell. Back at Dad's, I handed over the bolt so the farmer could pay and be on his way.

Next, I went to the employees' break area in the bolt room and bought an ice-cold, 10-ounce bottle of Pepsi from the pop machine. Then I ran out the side door of my dad's store and once again crossed a blazing-hot parking lot that led to my mom's store. At last, her customer was gone. I handed her the Pepsi as she listened to the 3 o'clock news on the radio, which began by naming the people who had been admitted to the local hospital the day before:

"April Bryant...Kevin Stackman...Peggy Larson..."

The announcer continued with the addresses of where dispatchers sent a police car or fire truck:

"...the 500 block of North Ash Street...the 1400 block of East Euclid Street."

For me, this was a typical summer day at my dad's store— sweeping the floor, running occasional errands, and generally goofing off. For my dad, the busy harvest season in large part determined whether Copeland Supply showed a profit or a loss for the entire year. And at 10 years old, I was too young to realize how precarious farming could be. Weather, of course, posed the greatest threat, especially given McPherson's location in the country's "tornado alley." More alarming, however, were events unfolding across the world that would in time reshape agriculture's entire industry, taking a toll on little towns like mine. No wonder there was a palpable urgency at my dad's hardware store.

It was my job to empty the trash and sweep the floor as retired farmers and oilfield workers mulled about to enjoy free coffee while cracking open peanuts. With my push broom, I attacked a relentless river of peanut shells, occasionally pausing to restock a metal peanut pan that was warmed by a 100-watt light bulb. I listened to "the coffee drinkers," as they were called, talk about the one and only thing they ever talked about: the weather. There was endless speculation about when it was supposed to rain and how much would come down. They talked about potential wind speeds and—God forbid—the possibility of hail, the arch enemy of wheat. Weather conditions today were compared to those from last year— and perhaps the summer 20 years ago when the crops were lost. They talked about how the scorching temperatures caused equipment to overheat, and they complained about muddy fields that bogged down the heavy harvesters and tractors. After hearing this for—just an estimate here—the zillionth time, I came to the conclusion that God invented weather for the sole purpose of giving farmers something to talk about.

The coffee drinkers dubbed me "Miss Nuisance," mainly because I inevitably interrupted their conversations with my push broom. But the nickname was all (or mostly, anyway) just in fun, because they also did nice things for me—like fixing flat tires on my bicycle and making me wood figurines and puzzles in their workshops.

Every now and then, Herb, one of the town's two undertakers, would come into Dad's store to join the retirees for a cup of coffee.

As he stood there shelling peanuts, one of the old farmers would invariably ask, "Hey, Herb, what-cha up to?" And the undertaker would respond, "Oh, I'm just stopping by to check in on my inventory."

Meanwhile, my dad and his two salesclerks, Jenny and Heyfae, hustled about to help the farmers find the pieces and parts they needed to get back to cutting their fields. While this played out, I couldn't help but imagine all of my friends hanging out in the snack bar at the city pool eating frozen Snickers bars. Or camping at Pete's Puddle. Or at the rodeo in Canton. Worse yet, I thought about my best friend Joanne, who was on a family vacation to Colorado. On vacation! In Colorado!

In truth, though, I liked being at my parents' stores because of all of the interesting people and things around me. Still, it would take awhile before I could be truly helpful. As a fourth grader, I was clumsy, like the time I knocked over a box of teeny-tiny upholstery tacks, scattering them everywhere. And my hand-me-down clothes—the curse of being the youngest child—did nothing to soften my tomboy looks. I was nothing like the clean-scrubbed Mennonite girls in pigtails and pressed dresses who often came into the store with their parents. To reassure me, my dad explained that I was deep in the throes of what he called the ugly years. "That's the phase all little girls go through," he said, "when their heads are too large, their teeth look funny, and their bodies are shaped like fire hydrants." He meant it to be comforting, truly, because he also called me "Miss America" when I got dressed up for church.

My sister and an older brother also worked at Mom and Dad's stores, sort of. Both of them had this uncanny ability to turn invisible whenever customers came in. Ricky was five years older than me and somewhat of a hardware prodigy. He knew all the different types of nuts, bolts, and screws by sight and could even rewire a broken lamp. Less adept was Karan, 16 months my senior. But she could at least fill out a sales ticket so a clerk could ring it up on the register. When I once tried to write up a ticket, my dad discovered some minor math errors, which relegated me back to broom duty. At the time, I thought he was such a stickler.

When business slowed, I broke away from my post by the coffee pot to goof off with Ricky—that is, if I could find him. I searched the bookkeeper's office and the paint room. I looked behind the auto parts counter and all throughout the bolt room. I couldn't find him in the little attic kitchenette where my dad made his lunch. That only left the back of the building, which held some storage rooms and the steel shop.

Going through the double doors, I was blasted by heat from the cutting torches and all sorts of terrifying machines that could snap, bend, drill, slice, and twist raw metal. The giant garage doors on each end of the shop were kept fully open, kindly letting in even more hot air. "Rhinestone Cowboy," the summer's big hit, spilled out of a radio tuned to KFDI. And there was Karan, perched on a desk, talking to one of the shop guys with "movie star hair," as my sister called it. Nearby, Cookie was manhandling a piece of flat iron on the drill press. (Cookie was my personal favorite ever since he came to coffee break and handed around a little plastic bag to his fellow employees. Inside was a kidney stone that he had passed earlier that morning.)

"Where's Ricky?" I asked my sister.

"He's in the alley testing traps," she said.

Ah, that's right. I forgot about the vermin. My dad and some of the customers had spotted an occasional rodent scurrying across the floor in the bolt room. Dad said he would give my brother 25 cents for every mouse that he caught. In typical fashion, Ricky decided he could literally build a better mousetrap than the manufactured ones sold at my father's store.

I walked outside to the alley, but also in typical fashion, my brother was nowhere in sight. Instead, I saw a row of Mason jars lined up alongside the building. Extra-chunky peanut butter, the bait, had been smeared deep inside the jars, and each one had been turned upside down and propped open with a little piece of cardboard. When a mouse wedged its little body under the lip of the jar to eat the peanut butter, it knocked over the cardboard prop, closing up the opening. My brother would show the trapped mouse to my father and collect his money. Any remaining peanut butter was scraped back into the jar to be reused in future traps. Sadly for me, the jar was stored next to the coffee pot. Feeling a little hungry one afternoon, I decided to snack on peanut butter and crackers. When my brother saw me slathering the recycled peanut butter onto a saltine, he slapped it out of my hand. Then he told me where the peanut butter came from, and I slapped him back.

In my youthful wisdom, I chose not to ask my father or my brother about the fate of the trapped mice. This, too, I learned the hard way. A year earlier, Dad and I were alone at his store after closing time. It was so quiet that we could hear a swishing sound in the other room. I followed him to the source of the noise: a mouse that had become trapped inside a metal trash can full of loose grass seed. Dad opened the lid, and he saw the mouse thrashing around in the seed, which he sold by the pound. He calmly closed the lid and walked to the checkout counter, with me trailing behind. There he doubled up two paper sacks and picked up a stapler. I followed him back to the can of grass seed and watched as he opened the lid and scooped the mouse into the sack. He folded over the end of the sack and stapled it shut. At this point, I had no idea what would happen next.

I followed my dad as he walked outside with the sealed paper sack. In one swift move, he dropped the sack on the ground and stomped on it, crushing the mouse. Dad didn't flinch when the mouse met its fate. Perhaps growing up on a farm, where hogs and chickens were the family's main source of meat, inured my father to distasteful tasks. That was not the case for me. I shrieked. I wept. I scolded. But then—and here comes the really twisted part—I begged him to open up the sack because I was curious to see the mouse guts inside. (He refused.) Even so, after that I didn't want to see any more bloodshed.

I had been in the shop for quite a while—so long, in fact, that I could hear my father hollering for Ricky, Karan, and me to come back up front. A number of previous messes and mishaps led Dad to believe that we needed a lot of adult supervision. He was right. Ricky was the ringleader in all sorts of pranks, games, and experiments. Wherever he went, trouble followed. And because my brother was so much fun, I became his eager assistant, no matter how foolish we were.

Re-entering the building through the steel shop, I crossed paths with George the Welder, a soft-spoken giant with a quiet little hee-hee laugh. Once, I was in the shop when the motorized garage door lift broke. The shop's forklift was unable to lift the garage door any higher than a few feet—not enough height for a freight truck to back into. As I marveled, George the Welder lumbered up to the door and lifted it up above his head, holding it aloft until someone propped it into place with a piece of metal pipe.

George knew that I wasn't supposed to be in the shop because it was so dangerous. But I loved poking around the long metal racks, which held all sizes and shapes of metal: flat iron, hollow square tubing, and cylindrical cold-rolled steel. He let me try on his welder's mask, which had a small, deeply-tinted window on the front, and his thick gloves, which almost reached my shoulders.

The steel shop closed at 5, while the hardware and auto parts counters were open until 6. I headed back to the front of the store and found that the coffee geezers had gone home for the day. But left in their wake was yet another batch of discarded peanut shells to sweep up. My last task of the day was emptying all of the trash cans throughout the store into big trash bags, which were loaded onto a flatbed cart. I rolled the cart to the dumpster in the alley. I was too short to open the lid of the dumpster and too weak to heave the bags of garbage over my head into it. So, my dad or one of the customers typically walked over to lend a hand.

When I finished with the trash, I ambled over to my mom's store. I found her standing next to the candy case chatting with a customer. Located next to the checkout counter, the candy case was a wooden cabinet with beveled glass on the front so customers could see the assorted sweets inside. I was partial to the chocolate-covered raisins. My sister liked the coconut haystacks. Mom bought the candy case with the idea the customers who were checking out would impulsively buy a bunch of candy to take home. But it didn't work out that way. Customers who were ready to pay for their purchases pointed at the case and asked to buy just one piece of chocolate. Mom put a small square of wax paper on the scale, and with little metal tongs she placed the chocolate on top. But instead of just paying the bill and going home, the customer ate the candy directly from the wax paper while talking to my mother. And to me, a kid, their conversations lasted— another estimate here—basically forever. I watched as the customer nibbled on a piece of white-chocolate bark and talked to Mom. It was a one-sided conversation that to me sounded like this: *"Blah, blah, blah blah. Blah, blah blah. Blah, blah, blah..."*

"Mom, can I go to the drugstore?" I interrupted.

"You need to say, 'Excuse me,'" she replied.

"Excuse me, Mom, can I go to the drugstore?"

"Yes, be careful."

Staying there any longer risked death by boredom. So, I left and rode my bike roughly three blocks south to a drugstore that, like my parents' stores, was located on Main Street. The pharmacy was in the back. In the space up front—amid the face creams and thermometers and hemorrhoid ointments—there was a soda fountain. People who visited the soda fountain were typically high schoolers who came in for, say, a vanilla Coke, or they were old men coming in for coffee. These were different old men drinking coffee than the old men who hung out at my dad's store drinking coffee. It always made me wonder, *What is it about old men and coffee?*

When I got there, only a few customers sat on the stools that lined the long counter and drank pop from tall glasses with crushed ice and straws. Behind the counter was my other brother, Ronnie, who was seven years older than me. He had been working at the drugstore for three years—ever since he started high school. As a soda jerk, Ronnie made each drink individually by mixing carbonated water with flavored syrup. I clambered up onto a stool—which was so high that my feet couldn't touch the floor. Without me asking, Ronnie mixed my favorite beverage: a Green River. As far as I could tell, a Green River was basically carbonated water mixed with lemon-lime syrup with bright green hue. But he was so methodical when he made one for me. First, he scooped crushed ice into a glass and dispensed the carbonated water into it. The syrup was added from a separate bottle and mixed in with a long teaspoon. A striped straw was the final touch before he slid the glass in front of me. When I drank a Green River that Ronnie made for me, my mouth filled up with little sunbeams.

My brother and I had a deal when I came into the drugstore. He didn't charge me for the Green River, but I had to buy him a package of Starbursts. It seemed fair to me, but looking back, I realize that he didn't pay for the Green River either.

Refreshed, I mounted my bicycle and headed back to my dad's store. It was closing time, and Heyfae was counting out the money in the cash register behind the front counter. Her name was really just Fae, but customers said "Hey, Fae" when they greeted her, and somehow the two words permanently ran together.

Jenny counted out the money in the cash register behind the auto parts counter. In the past, the auto parts clerk counted out his cash register, but his amount in the drawer wasn't matching the total sales. Nobody could understand why it occasionally came up short. My father didn't suspect theft, saying this clerk was "as honest as a day is long." This man worked Monday through Friday and a half-day on Saturday. Then on Sunday he served as the pastor of a small, charismatic church in town. I attended services there once or twice because it was just down the street from our house. The church had fewer than 30 members, but they could sure belt out the hymns. I discovered that the pastor—the man I knew as the auto-parts clerk—possessed the God-given gift of "speaking in tongues." During a particularly fiery sermon, he was overcome with emotion, and his words became incomprehensible and to me sounded like babble. Perhaps someone in the congregation had the God-given gift of discerning words spoken in tongues, but not me. My family went to the Baptist church, but our services were a little more subdued.

While the auto-parts clerk was clearly a passionate preacher, he may not have been as gifted when it came to handling money. The store's cash register was likely coming up short because he was giving incorrect change and/or ringing up returned merchandise as a sale rather than a refund.

As Jenny and Heyfae counted out, they wrote down the number of pennies, nickels, dimes, and quarters, as well as the number of bills in their cash-register drawer. All of the coins and some of the bills remained in the registers' drawers, ready for business the next day. The rest of the money—along with personal checks and credit-card slips—went into a zippered bank bag that was put in the safe. This was a nightly ritual. Jenny and Heyfae counted out the cash registers, while Dad went to his attic kitchenette to drink a Salty Dog from a mayonnaise jar. A Salty Dog is grapefruit juice and vodka that Dad stirred together with his index finger. He said he only drank upstairs so the Baptists wouldn't see him. I found that reasoning somewhat confusing. *He belonged to the Baptist church, but knowingly broke its rules*, I thought.

Finally, the lights were shut off and the burglar alarm was set. Dad locked the safe and it was time to go home. Across the parking lot, Mom counted out her cash register, but before doing so, she took a quarter from her purse to replace the quarter I took out for her afternoon Pepsi. That way, the money in the cash register would match the total cash sales for the day. (At the end of the month, my parents exchanged business checks, with Dad paying for the 1/4 x

3 bolt and any other merchandise "borrowed" from Mom's store. Mom's check covered any merchandise borrowed from Dad's store.)

Mom turned off the lights, locked her front door, and headed home. Later that night, the "door shaker" from the police department walked down both sides of Main Street, pulling on the door handles of every store to make sure all the merchants remembered to secure their buildings.

At 6:30, I was far too tired to ride my bike the incredibly long distance between the stores and our house, roughly five city blocks.

"I'm exhausted," I whined. "I can hardly move."

"All that sweeping can sure wear a person out," my father teased. "Somehow you weren't too tired to ride your bike to the drugstore."

"Dad, pleeeeaaaasssseee!" I begged.

I knew all along he was just kidding me, because Dad loaded my bike into the back of his pickup and drove me home.

By the time we got there, Mom's car was already in the driveway. Ronnie had finished his shift at the drugstore, and both he and Ricky were in their bedrooms. Karan was in the bedroom that she and I shared. Her side was piled high with dirty clothes, food wrappers, and the remnants of some random craft project. My side featured a neatly-made bed and a bookshelf with Nancy Drew mystery books alphabetized by title.

"You better stay on your side of the masking tape!" I hollered out to her.

Meanwhile, Mom rushed to make supper. On the menu: hamburger casserole, a recipe from the First Baptist Church cookbook. First, Mom browned some beef in a skillet while boiling elbow macaroni in a saucepan. After draining both the meat and the macaroni, she combined the two, along with some salt, pepper, and a can of condensed cream of tomato soup. Next—and this was a brilliant twist invented by my mother—she added a can of condensed cream of mushroom soup. The mixture became extra gooey, which Mom said "made it classy." Everything was dumped into a casserole dish that I buttered for her. I meticulously removed the cellophane wrappers from six slices of American cheese and placed them atop the hamburger-macaroni mixture. The whole shebang went into the oven for what seemed like a staggeringly long time, but probably for 30 minutes.

That was just enough time for Mom to make a salad and for me to set the table: place mats, silverware, glasses, and napkins for six people. And, as always, a little plate with a stack of white bread and a tub of margarine. By 7:30, I was so hungry I could eat my toenails. But before we could eat, my siblings and I each had to say a prayer. One by one, we recited the same words: "Dear Lord, thank you for this food. Glad we have homes, schools, and churches. Amen." The salad bowl went around the table, and we passed our plates to Dad for a heaping spoonful of the casserole. Now, here's the part that always galled me. As if on purpose, my dad plunked a spoonful of piping hot casserole onto my plate—but it was *touching my lettuce.* When I complained, Dad said, "Bethy, it's going to be that way in your stomach anyway." Then Ronnie, who rarely piped up, came to my defense, telling Dad, "You know, milk goes sour in your stomach. But that doesn't mean you want to drink sour milk." Touché, Ronnie!

In the half-hour spent eating, Ricky and I were able to taunt Karan to the point that she either became enraged and stormed off, or broke down into loud sobbing. It all depended on her mood that day. Razzing my sister was a kind of sport for us because she was so emotional. Her classmates also teased her mercilessly, in part because her body had developed so quickly. At 11, Karan had already outgrown her training bra.

Once I took my taunting too far. After school one day, I wanted to use the pay phone to ask my mom to come pick me up. There was only one pay phone in the entire school, and a weird kid we called Kirk the Jerk was on it. Every time we drove by his house, he stood on the curb and pretended to throw rocks at our car.

Kirk was yacking on and on, taking forever. I felt that because he was hogging the phone, it was entirely my right to tell him to hang up so I could use the phone myself. But when I snapped at him, he held his hand over the mouthpiece and called me a name. I had never heard the word before, but being from farm country I was pretty sure it had something to do with a chicken.

I stashed the word away in my verbal arsenal, knowing that the supper table was the perfect place to put it to use. One night, Ricky and I were taunting Karan in all the usual ways—and I had my chance to unleash my new word. I blurted out to my sister, "You cocksucker!"

It did not have the intended effect.

Suddenly, the supper table got very quiet. My parents stared at me in disbelief, blinking their eyes slowly, like cows in a pasture. Clearly, they had never heard the word either, and I patiently explained that it referred to a chicken. They, along with my brothers and sister, disagreed. Not only did they refuse to tell me what the word meant, but I was excused from the table, even though I hadn't finished my Jell-O.

Tonight, happily, there were no sibling squabbles. After supper was over, Karan had to help clean up because I had helped prepare the meal and set the table. Then, she wandered off to our bedroom. I tried to rustle up the cat, Doorknob, who darted off when he spotted me coming toward him. The more I tried to get Doorknob to love me, the farther he ran. (My dad hated Doorknob because the cat frequently gave him "the old one-eye" when the cat turned his butt at him.) Ricky headed to his room to take apart a radio that he might or might not eventually reassemble.

"I'm soooooo bored," I complained to my mother. "There's nothing to do here. We never get to have any fun."

"That's not true," my mother said. "You played mini golf with your friends just a few days ago."

That had slipped my mind, but my overall argument was still valid. "I forgot about that, but even so, that doesn't happen very often," I whined.

"Aren't you going skating with the youth group on Sunday?" she asked again.

She had a point there. The church's youth pastor occasionally took us on outings to the skating rink and bowling alley in town. "Yes, but it's always the same old people there," I retorted weakly.

"And what about Bob Hope?"

With that, my mother won our dispute.

Recently, a woman walked into my mother's store carrying a stack of slick-looking promotional posters. She told us she was a marketing representative from Wichita, and was in McPherson to tout an upcoming appearance by the legendary comedian Bob Hope at the Kansas Coliseum. I had seen the entertainer on TV, and even as a kid I thought he was pretty funny. But Ricky and Karan merely saw Hope as a has-been from the World War II era.

The woman showed my mother the poster, telling her that if she agreed to hang one in her front window, she would get one free ticket to Bob Hope's show. Without saying so, Mom realized that the woman was offering just one ticket because she was confident that Mom would pay $25 to buy a second ticket for my father, who also happened to be a big fan of the comedian. But Mom had a better idea. "I'd be happy to hang the poster in my window," my mother said. "And if you go to the store next door, I bet that owner there would agree to hang one as well." The marketing woman said she would give it a try, not knowing that the owner next door was my dad. That night at the supper table, my father proudly held up his free ticket to Bob Hope's show. Then, because my mother was kind and generous and loved me dearly, she replied, "I also have a free ticket to see Bob Hope. And I'm giving it to Bethy, because she wants to go too."

By playing the Bob Hope trump card, my mother had made it clear that I had plenty of things to do. My only response was, "Why can't we get cable TV like everyone else? We're stuck with, like, four channels."

Exasperated, my mother said, "Maybe it's a good time to go outside and play."

When it got dark, I got Ricky and Karan to help me round up some neighborhood kids for a game of kick the can. I prided myself on finding ingenious hiding places around sheds and shrubs by nearby houses. But being so tucked away made for a long-distance sprint to kick the coffee can over before "It" could tag me. Neighborhood games were about my only expression of athletic prowess. None of the Copeland kids went out for team sports at school—even in a state where basketball was more of a religion than a sport. Nor did we particularly follow professional teams like the Kansas City Chiefs and the Royals on TV. In truth, our family life revolved around those two hardware stores. A "big win" for us was getting a large order, making payroll, or mailing out the monthly statements on time.

Ronnie didn't join us for kick the can. In fact, he didn't spend much time at the stores or even at home with us. Many times after supper, he would get in his Chevy and head downtown to "drag Main," which was a big deal in McPherson. Pretty much every evening in the summer, teenagers loaded up their cars with their friends and drove up and down Main Street, starting at Dairy Queen on the south end and turning around at the Gibson's discount store on the north end.

Since pickup trucks—seemingly the official vehicle of McPherson High School—had bench seats, a girl could scoot over and sit next to the boy who was driving. The first time I saw that, I asked my dad why the girl was scooted next to the boy. Dad said, "Why, Bethy, he's giving her driving lessons." It made sense to me at the time, actually. A beginner would need to watch the dashboard dials and foot pedals when learning to drive.

All down Main Street, there was lots of shouting and laughing between the cars, especially when they were stopped at traffic lights. Who was riding in what cars revealed an unspoken pecking order, with the cute jocks and cheerleaders grouped at the top.

Ronnie was not a jock, nor was he terribly cute. But he made custom sodas at the drugstore, which earned him a high spot in the pecking order.

Back at home, Mom took her usual place at the end of the supper table. There, she shuffled a deck of cards to play a few hands of solitaire, stopping every now and then to take a drag from her cigarette. As she laid out the cards, she looked ahead to the following day: unloading a freight delivery, sending in her quarterly taxes, meeting with a bride-to-be to make her bridal registry.

Even today, when I picture Mom at home, this is where she is seated. It is here that she is happiest—the modest ranch-style home that she and Dad built shortly after coming to McPherson. Given a choice, Mom would be perfectly content at her store or in her house—and nowhere else.

In her heart, she believed that God had answered her most desperate prayers: She had a home of her own and a husband who loved her. In this place, she could give her children the happy memories that she herself never enjoyed.

For me, knowing how terrible it once was for Mom helped explain why she put in so many hours at her store. She wanted a better life for her kids, obviously. But she also wanted a better life for *herself*.

As Mom smoked and shuffled the cards, Dad puttered outside. He had built a large shed in our backyard that reminded him of the barn at his home in East Texas, where he grew up during the Great Depression. Stacked high in one half of his shed was all the random stuff that he said was not good enough for the house, but too good for the city dump. The other side had a little workshop exclusively for his own use, and much like the bolt room at his store, he was the only one who could find anything in there.

Along the sidewalk leading from the back door of the house to the barn were giant buckets that once held long, heavy lengths of chain that he sold by the foot at his store. Each held a tomato or pepper plant, and Dad tenderly fussed over each one. Next, he filled the bird feeder with fresh seed and put an ear of dried corn on the squirrel feeder, which was designed so that the squirrel had to sit in a little chair with its elbows on a table to eat the corn. This was the extent of our garden.

We once had billowing mounds of climbing roses, but my mom made my dad take them out because the "trellis" was actually an old box spring that had been stripped clean for the roses to climb. Mom didn't think it was classy enough.

As much as anything, these evening rituals exemplify how my parents operated. Even though they were happily married and raising kids, they worked independently.

My folks didn't set out to operate separate, side-by-side hardware stores. It just happened that way. Even today I'm not sure why they had to own two different businesses, but I'm guessing that Mom couldn't work with Dad, and Dad couldn't work with Mom. So, each store was independently run, and my parents concealed from each other any details of sales, expenses, inventory, and earnings.

A family photo for the church directory shows Ronnie, Ricky, Karan, and me with Mom and Dad in the early 1970s.

Maybe it came down to this: Both of my parents grew up poor. That alone made them eager to succeed in business—so they could have nice things for themselves and us kids. But having two stores was a kind of insurance policy for them. Like, if one store didn't make it, maybe the other one would.

Beth DeCarbo

2.
THE SUMMER OF 1944

Waiting on the platform, Gene and his father stood rigidly next to a single suitcase, eyes fixed on train tracks that shimmered in the harsh summer sun of East Texas.

Mute, stone-faced, they dared not let their eyes meet. Instead, father and son stared into the distance, willing the locomotive into the depot.

Today, I'm sending a third son off to war, Allen thought. *When will it end?*

As his father fretted, Gene tried to hide his excitement. At 18 and a recent graduate of Palestine High School's Class of 1944, his adventure was just beginning. On August 1, a letter had arrived in the mail that read: "Greetings from the President of the United States, Franklin D. Roosevelt." He had been drafted into World War II.

Gene's entire life up until then had been spent working. He had regular duties on the family's farm, plus a side job before and after school—all just to help his parents and seven siblings get by.

On the threshold of his new life, Gene's thoughts drifted to his old one.

"We were poor before the Depression, we were poor during the Depression, and we are poor after the Depression," he mused. Now it will be up to three of his younger brothers—James, George, and Bill—to help keep the family going.

His sister Eleanor—who the family called Tootsie—helped her mother inside the house and was busy at school. And the youngest son, John, was considered "simple" and could contribute little to the family finances. Since prenatal care and advanced diagnostics weren't options for the family, they were left to guess why John was mentally disabled. Gene theorized that John didn't get enough oxygen during childbirth at home. Another sibling thought it was because John fell from a tree and cracked his skull when he was a toddler. The children's mother, Lockie, blamed two of her own children for the disability, saying that Edward, the oldest, was trying to chase down Harold, the second oldest, with a horse, which put her into early labor.

Gene's thoughts were interrupted by the sound of rumbling in the distance. He and the other ticket holders on the platform craned their necks to spot the approaching train. Meanwhile, Allen looked down and shuffled his feet.

There won't be any long speeches from my father, Gene thought. Even with eight rambunctious children, he's a quiet man, never argumentative. *'Pshaw' is the worst word he'll ever use.*

With a whoosh and a screech, the train pulled into the depot. Gene picked up his suitcase with his left hand, and with his right, he reached out to his father. Then, the two men shook hands. It was a brief, casual exchange, like between in-laws at a church picnic. There was no lack of love by any means. But nobody would ever accuse a Copeland of showing too much affection.

The train eventually took Gene to Amarillo, Texas, located in the state's panhandle—easily the farthest from home he had ever been. As a newly-drafted soldier in the U.S. Army Air Corps, he knew he was headed to basic training, but beyond that, his new life was a mystery to him.

Exhausted from the long trip, Gene faced another trip upon arrival at the depot. Buses were lined up to take him and other draftees to a new air base the Army Air Corps had built just east of the city limits. Scanning the aircraft on the grounds, his mission became clearer.

"I bet we're going to work on B-17s," he said to the man next to him.

Gene was right. Called the Flying Fortress, the Boeing B-17 was a fast, heavily-armed aircraft that could carry up to two tons of bombs. Learning to work on airplanes was a perfect fit for him, Gene thought, even though he had never flown in an airplane in his life.

Most of his early education took place in a one-room schoolhouse near the farm. There, his buddies called him "Shang" because he was as thin as a shingle (which in a Texas drawl is pronounced "shangle"). But in high school, much of his time was spent taking vocational-agricultural classes. That's where he learned the basics of mechanics and how to operate various types of machinery.

Gene's stint in Amarillo was brief, with little time to make lasting friendships. Considering his shyness, it was hard for him to make friends in the first place. For proof, one could look at his high school senior yearbook. There were no inscriptions written in the front or back covers, and few mentions of school activities. Next to his senior picture was one line: "Ears like cab doors."

After several months in Amarillo, Gene shipped out to Gulfport, Mississippi, where the War Department had commissioned a hangar at the Army Air Field to accommodate the larger Boeing B-29s, which were dubbed the Superfortress.

In Gulfport, Gene and the other new arrivals attended airplane mechanics school to learn to work on B-29s, which had what at the time was considered state-of-the-art technology. There were many similarities to the B-17s, but they also had advanced features, including pressurized cabins. When classes ended, disappointment awaited him.

"We have been put on a production line!" Gene complained in a letter to his mother. "I do the same job every day, all day: change the No. 3 spark plugs in engines. It is very monotonous."

The military kept the mechanics busy, so Gene's off-duty life was monotonous too. In the barracks, his buddies taught him to play a card game called casino, and while money changed hands, he wasn't a high-roller player.

As for dating, "I'm pretty shy as far as girls go," he wrote to his mother. "And besides, I just don't have time." In closing, he assured her, "Even though I'm far from home, I don't feel lonely or homesick."

Now that he was earning a good paycheck, Gene was able to include small sums of money in his letters that his father could someday use to build a grocery store for the two of them to own and operate. The residual effects of the Dust Bowl and increasingly modern farming methods were making Allen Copeland's tenant farm unfeasible in supporting the family.

Separately, Gene wrote his sister Tootsie once a month and included $15 in the envelope so she could have some spending money.

On September 2, 1945, Japan formally surrendered aboard the USS Missouri, signifying the Allied victory and the end of World War II. Soon after, Gene was discharged from the service, and he was free to leave Gulfport to go home to Palestine. But he knew he faced a lot of competition for jobs from other GIs.

Even though the war was over, the country still needed troops, and Gene was offered a deal. If he re-upped into the Army of Occupation, he would get a $300 bonus, a 30-day furlough, and a stripe to the rank of private first class.

So, Gene re-enlisted, confident that his next deployment would also involve aircraft mechanics. He just didn't know where.

Once again, he and the other enlistees were put on a train, this time to Kearns, Utah. After a few weeks of drills and skills assessment, Gene got his first clue of what was to come.

"I drew all winter clothes: parkas, winter boots, thick blankets," he wrote his mother.

It would be his last letter to her for a very long time.

The men were loaded onto a troop carrier and flown to Seattle. The following day, his squadron boarded an old excursion boat called the David W. Branch for a long, pitched trip across the open sea.

The next morning, as he swung from a hammock in a fetid hold below deck, Gene moaned to his sergeant, "I'm so sick, I can't hold my head up."

Anyone in the Copeland family could have vouched for him. Even the shortest, flattest car ride could lead to violent wretching.

After 21 miserable days at sea, Gene landed in Shemya, a small island in the chain of Aleutians far off the coast of Alaska. There, he lived in a Quonset hut embedded in the snow. "It was the coldest winter of my life," he later told his sister.

He was initially assigned to work on airplanes, but his ability as a jack-of-all-trades broadened his job description.

"I can do a little bit of everything," he told his commanding officer.

As a result, his duties took him all over the island. He was the squadron barber and movie projectionist; he was given a motor pool with a few trucks to look after; he distributed both the beer and liquor rations and occasionally cans of Campbell's soup, coffee, crackers, and cheese to get the men through "williwaw" storms that could last up to 10 days. In the process, he earned a little spending money in a gray-market for food and liquor.

Gene left active duty in the Army Air Corps on October 31, 1946. He had arrived on Shemya as a private first class and left as a sergeant. Even though he was returning to civilian life, he signed up for the Air Force Reserve, knowing he could be recalled to service later.

Gene was sent back to San Antonio and made his way home to Palestine. By that time, his father had quit farming and purchased a small grocery store on the outskirts of town. The ramshackle building was torn down, and a new store was built in its place. Even though they had agreed to work together as 50-50 partners, Gene told his father that in the long term, "This little store won't make enough to support two families."

One day, a customer came into the store and mentioned that

oilman Sid Richardson had plans to build a big gasoline plant outside of Kermit, Texas. Richardson was well known in West Texas as a "wildcat driller"—meaning he gambled on striking oil in areas not known to be oil fields.

Gene applied and got a job that would send him to Kermit and Odessa, Texas. That meant he would be moving away from home again.

"I like having my own job," he told his parents. "Jobs are scarce. I'll be working and finally independent."

His boss was Gaines Billue, who went by "Smokey," and Gene's assignment was to maintain the instruments on oil wells across the Permian Basin, taking readings and changing charts on 300 different wells.

The job with the Sid Richardson Co. lasted until 1950, when Gene was called back into service during the Korean War. This stint would take him to Shreveport, Louisiana, where he was once again working on B-29s. But this time, his commanding officers gave him more challenging assignments, such as RB-35s, small reconnaissance bombers.

"Every casual plane that came in, I can work on too," he wrote in his letters home. "They found out I had a little more ability than most guys. I had learned how to do a lot of things—by living on a farm, working for Billue, and in the oilfields."

When that stint was up on October 9, 1951, he went back to Kermit to get his job back. There he was told, "You're fired!"

Apparently, the irascible Billue had angered the higher ups at the Sid Richardson Co., and he and his whole crew were axed.

So Billue quit to pursue his novel idea of "underground storage," in which salt is dissolved deep in the earth to create caverns to store petroleum products.

Gene reconnected with Billue, who gave him a job. For his first assignment in 1952, Gene was told to drive to a place three miles west of McPherson, Kansas, and meet up with a man who would give him further instructions.

When he got to the designated place, he saw a man sitting on top of a bulldozer.

"What's going on?" Gene asked.

"I'm waiting for some son-of-a-bitch from Texas to come and take over," the man said.

"I am that son-of-a-bitch," Gene replied.

The man's first name was James, but he went by "Foots." Together, Gene and Foots core drilled—that is, extracted samples of earth far beneath its surface—to identify salt formations. Then, Gene devised a way to make caverns in the salt deposits that would be used for storing liquid petroleum gas (LPG) inside them. Propane and butane are major components of LPG, and up until then, they had mostly been burned off during the refining process. Billue and Gene realized that an enormous source of energy was going to waste.

Work commenced on Well No. 1, the first well to be installed in Kansas and probably one of the first 25 wells in the world, Gene would write years later in his personal history of underground storage.

Gaines "Smokey" Billue dispatched Gene to McPherson for the first time in 1952. There, he was instructed to devise a way to create salt caverns underground for storing petroleum products.

In 1954, Billue got a contract to drill an experimental well for storing fuel in shale (instead of salt). The drilling site: Gallup, New Mexico. And Billue, Gene, his brother George, and the rest of the crew took rooms at the famed El Rancho Hotel. Of course, Gene didn't know it at the time, but staying at the El Rancho would change the trajectory of his life.

Located on old U.S. Route 66, the El Rancho was built by R.E. Griffith, the brother of film director D.W. Griffith. The resort hosted some of Hollywood's biggest names—Robert Mitchum, Elia Kazan, Spencer Tracy, and Katharine Hepburn, among others.

Gallup was one of the larger cities in New Mexico at the time, even though it had just over 9,000 residents. And its location along Route 66 bolstered tourism, making it a glamorous destination that embodied America's romanticized version of the Wild West.

No one will ever know for sure, but there is a chance that on the day that Gene Copeland checked into the El Rancho Hotel, Betty Carey—his future wife—was just steps away in the dining room.

Betty had been working at the resort for roughly two years when Billue's crew came to town. Pictures of her during this period show her in fashionable clothing with beautifully coiffed hair and lipstick. Her smart looks belied a harrowing past. She had fled to Gallup from a difficult marriage in Lordsburg to man she wed when she was just 16 years old. She left behind a baby boy, who was being raised by his grandparents.

Even before that, Betty's life had been marked by heartache and suffering, starting with the tragic loss of her mother when Betty was just five years old. In moving to Gallup, Betty was determined to start a new life for herself—and to avoid men like the one who had caused so much sorrow for her in her earlier marriage.

At the El Rancho, one of these bums had already propositioned Betty, who was quick to turn him down. The man's name was Elvis Presley, a singer who was still somewhat of a nobody back then. The dining room at the El Rancho had a large stage for live performances, and Elvis was booked as one of the acts. At some point during his gig, Elvis had a crew member take a note to Betty, asking her to meet him after his show that night.

When a co-worker saw the note, she asked Betty what she told Elvis.

"I told him no, of course!" Betty said.

"Really? I think he's kind of cute," her friend replied.

In a voice filled with disgust, Betty dismissed the idea. "He's such a slob!" she exclaimed. "He wipes his nose on his sleeve."

Knowing that she rejected Elvis for his piggish manners, it's surprising that Betty didn't snub Gene after seeing him return from the oilfields covered from head to toe in dust and grime.

Still, he must have cleaned up nicely, because an offhand remark led to a first date.

"I know a cute gal you might like," one of the drillers on the crew told Gene.

After some introductions, Betty agreed to go out with Gene. Afterward—but without using these exact words—Gene told the other driller that he was smitten.

The shale-drilling project kept Gene and the crew in Gallup for two or three months until the weather got too cold for field work. Gene and his brother George returned to Palestine and helped their father build the new grocery store. By then, Betty must have been smitten too.

At home, Gene's sister Tootsie could see a change in her brother. One clue was all of the letters coming to him postmarked Gallup. Gene confided that he was in love, sheepishly admitting, "She is quite prolific in writing, I can say that."

Gene asked Tootsie to help him pick out an engagement ring, which was sent to Betty in the U.S. mail. When his sister asked why he didn't wait to propose in person, Gene replied, "I want to let her have it so she can show it off, I guess."

Obviously, Betty didn't mind the long-distance proposal because she wrote back and said, "Yes."

Meanwhile, Gene went to Tishomingo, Oklahoma, to work on another project with Billue. To say that Billue was difficult would be like calling the Grand Canyon a pothole. He was a kind of mad genius, but also an impossible boss with mood swings that made him completely unpredictable.

He could be carefree and jocular one day, and surly and snappish the next. But no matter his mood, Billue was always tight-fisted when it came to money.

"Make sure you get paid what you're owed," Gene told his brother George after every oilfield project.

In fact, it came as no surprise to George how difficult Billue made it for Gene and Betty to get hitched.

"I told Billue I was getting married, and he told me not to," Gene told his brother. "I insisted, and he took me to the Wichita Falls airport and handed me a ticket—which was my paycheck. I found out before I got on the plane that the ticket was absolutely worthless, so I had to buy my own plane ticket to Albuquerque and only had $16 left in my pocket. When I got to the train depot in Albuquerque for a ride to Gallup, it was full. So, I went around the gate through an opening in the fence. I didn't get caught until toward the end of the trip, when the conductor asked me for my ticket. I said I only had $16, and he said that would do. When I got to Gallup, Betty said, 'I'm sure glad you got here, because I was going to get married tonight—even if I had to marry the best man.'"

Somehow it worked out, and Gene and Betty were wed on June 23, 1954, in Clovis, New Mexico, which Gene chose because his parents had gotten married there decades earlier. The newly-minted Copelands—he was 28, she was 23—honeymooned at a motel owned by the same people who owned the El Rancho.

"We got the bridal suite and a big bowl of fruit," Gene recounted to his brother.

Shortly after the wedding, Gene and Betty moved to Wichita Falls, Texas, where Gene helped build a gasoline plant, earning $200 a month.

"That's all Billue is paying me!" he told George.

Betty got a job waiting tables at the Kemp Hotel in Wichita Falls, which made Gene grumble a bit because he didn't want his wife working. But her earnings, in part, kept the newlyweds afloat.

The couple traveled to the Piney Woods of East Texas so Betty could meet the big, boisterous Copeland clan. But before they arrived, Gene and Betty agreed to keep Betty's early life—her divorce and the baby she bore—a secret. It was the 1950s, when things like that were seen as scandalous in "good families."

Like his brothers, Gene had a big personality and was somewhat of a character—with none of the shyness and quiet reserve seen in his youth. At any family gathering, the Copeland brothers entertained the family with a steady stream of funny stories and jokes.

"We were so poor, that at Christmastime, our parents cut holes in our pockets so we'd have something to play with," George told Betty.

She didn't get the joke at first, probably because she didn't grow up in a house full of boys. So, Gene had to explain it to her later.

But George went on to tell Betty a true story that helped her better understand the family's humble background.

"One year, when I was about five or so, it was my birthday," he recalled. "My mother polished a nickel and dropped it into a pan of cake batter. The cake was baked, frosted, and sliced. When the pieces were served to everyone in the family, somehow my piece magically had the nickel inside of it. That nickel was my birthday present that year."

When the gasoline plant was completed in Wichita Falls, Billue had another project in mind. And this one would take Gene and Betty to McPherson for good, ending what had been a transient, touch-and-go existence for Betty. Coming to McPherson also put Betty on the road to success—but that would come much later. Ironically, "Betty didn't want to come at first," Gene recounted later.

But she didn't have a choice. McPherson had the one thing Smokey Billue needed to make Security Underground Storage a viable business venture: a refinery.

3.
THE EMERALD CITY

At nighttime, you can't miss the refinery from Exit 60 on Interstate 135. The sprawling facility is brightly lit up, just like the Emerald City in *The Wizard of Oz*. McPherson is a continental crossroads located in the heart of the Great Plains. Before this place even had a name, thousands of frontier pioneers in covered wagons cut through McPherson on the Santa Fe Trail en route to New Mexico. Later, massive cattle drives that started in Texas followed the Chisholm Trail as it cut through McPherson County on the way to the railhead in Abilene, Kansas, just to the northeast. In 1872, the town fathers made McPherson official, naming it after a Civil War general, James Birdseye McPherson. Not once did the Union Army hero step foot inside the city limits. (That's likely because he was dead, killed almost a decade earlier in the Battle of Atlanta.)

When Gene and Betty moved to town in 1956, they stayed at the Warren Hotel, a four-story brick building across the street from the courthouse. It was owned by the Smith family, and old man Smitty managed the front desk, which featured a display case with candy bars, cigars, and chewing tobacco. If a guest wanted to go upstairs, old man Smitty would scoot around the display case to escort the guest into the elevator. Then, he'd close the elevator door and interior accordion cage door before selecting the appropriate floor to ascend. That regimen was reversed to return to the lobby, so old man Smitty could hustle back behind the front desk.

A restaurant inside the hotel served reliable meat-and-three meals and was a popular destination for the locals after Sunday church services. Gene had already met a few folks from his previous stints in town working for Billue. In fact, it was a recent acquaintance at the Warren Hotel who taught Gene an important lesson: the proper way to pronounce the name of the town.

Like most newcomers, Gene made the mistake of referring to McPherson as Mac-FEAR-son. He did this at supper one evening, and a man sitting in a nearby booth was kind enough to correct him: "There's no FEAR, in Mc-FUR-son!"

After a few weeks at the Warren Hotel, Gene and Betty found a small house to rent located five blocks east of Main Street. Like many post-war wives, Betty was a full-time homemaker who cooked and cleaned and taught herself to use a sewing machine. Meanwhile, Gene continued to go to work, creating salt caverns underground to store petroleum products.

The job was challenging and could be dangerous because of the heavy machinery and materials, not to mention the highly flammable petroleum products. Gene never lost a crew member, but in rare cases, someone might lose part or all of a finger, for example.

While Gene was managing the oilfield work, he was also managing the increasingly-erratic Billue. His boss's latest idea was to raise sunken boats by injecting their hulls with ping pong balls. Gene declined to take on that challenge, knowing that it was just another one of Billue's wild-hair schemes.

Back on the home front, he and Betty were nearly finished with construction on a two-bedroom, ranch-style home in the new part of town. It was completed in early 1958 and decorated with a few choice pieces of Mid-Century Modern furniture, which was all the rage. A full set of china—which included matching cigarette lighters and ashtrays—was purchased at the Kansas State Fair. Shortly after moving in, they had their first son, Ron.

"If it weren't for the baby, I'd quit today," Gene told Betty.

Lately, he had been tussling with Billue to get paid for contractual work they had agreed upon. Their latest project was a five-year contract with the Defense Department to build and operate a six-well storage system for jet fuel.

In 1960, Gene and Betty had another baby, whom they named Rick. Their house was feeling a little cramped at this point, prompting them to build a two-bedroom addition. With a bigger house payment and another mouth to feed, Gene was feeling the squeeze.

It's not to say that the young couple wasn't happy. They took square-dancing lessons and belonged to a bridge club. Gene enrolled in night classes at one of McPherson's two small liberal arts colleges, and he sat on the board of the Y.M.C.A. And like pretty much every God-fearing family in the Eisenhower era, they joined a church.

By 1963, however, Gene had reached his breaking point.

"I quit," he told Betty point-blank after work one night. "Billue is crazy."

Coincidentally, on the day that Gene unexpectedly quit, Betty had a surprise for him.

"I'm pregnant," she announced.

Making financial matters worse, earlier that same day, Betty had purchased a new upright piano on credit. With two children at home and a third on the way, Gene couldn't afford to be unemployed. Luckily, it didn't take long for the refinery to hire him as a consultant, paying $1,000 a month.

Karan was born in December 1963, just a couple of weeks after John F. Kennedy's assassination. By now, Ron was five and Rick was three. They had already lived through both the threat of nuclear war with Russia and the thrill of a spaceship orbiting Earth.

The world is changing so fast, Betty thought. *What's in store for these babies?*

As for Gene, the refinery ordered work to begin on wells No. 31 through 37, each with a capacity of 30,000 barrels. But while crews did the heavy work, Gene was relegated to a desk, far from the action in the field.

"I'm so bored," he complained to Betty. "I'm in the office all day, every day—just sitting there in case something goes wrong."

About this time, a banker friend told Gene about a business he might be interested in.

"There's a junkyard on the west end of town," he said. "It mainly takes in scrap metal and other oilfield salvage, and you know a lot of people in that line of business. The junkyard also has a metal-fabrication shop, so there's an opportunity to grow."

Later in life, Gene would tell his children: "Never trust a banker." But for now, he listened.

He bought the junkyard, naming his business Copeland Supply. In addition to oilfield salvage—pipe, old pump jacks, derricks—he bought and salvaged a decommissioned Atlas missile base that was constructed at the height of the country's Cold War. And he also salvaged scrap from farmers who hauled in old metal tools and machinery that they no longer wanted.

In 1965, Gene and Betty gave birth to their fourth and final child, whom they named Elizabeth. She was born breech with jet black hair and would grow up to become her parents' favorite child. Being that baby and the sole author of this book, I am allowed this shameless literary license.

Around this time, my parents were seeing the first glimpses of Rick's impishness. It started when he set the living room carpet on fire. Luckily, it was extinguished before too much damage was done. Later, though, things got out of hand—literally.

When I was a toddler, I was playing on the floor next to a bedroom door. Rick was horsing around, and he inadvertently slammed the door on my middle finger, cutting off the tip. Hearing my screams, my father rushed over to see the stump of my finger squirting blood with my every heartbeat.

My mother wasn't at home at the time, so Dad called a neighbor, who was a registered nurse.

"I have the end of her finger in my hand, and she's bleeding everywhere," he told her. "What should I do?"

Then, with all the training and experience of someone who has long worked in the medical field, the neighbor said, "TAKE HER TO THE EMERGENCY ROOM NOW!"

The ER doctor couldn't reattach the tip of my finger, so today it's just a little shorter than it should be, and the nail curves over the end. Unless somebody looks closely, it's not noticeable, but nonetheless, Ricky would apologize whenever the subject came up.

With four small children, my mother was a traditional stay-at-home mom. For Easter, she sewed new outfits for me and my sister and purchased frilly matching hats. Christmas was a big deal with homemade candy and lots of decorations, including a shiny tinsel Christmas tree wrapped with twinkling lights.

In the early days, Karan, Ricky, and I went to the hardware stores
after school, and we played all sorts of cutthroat games,
one of which involved roofing nails.

For my birthday, invitations had to be mailed to every kid in my class so nobody would feel excluded. The party started in the backyard with a spirited game of Pin the Tail on the Donkey or Red Rover. I banned dodge ball because the boys threw the ball too hard, leading to welts on my legs. Inside, the family room was decorated with balloons and crepe paper streamers. We sat on the floor at a long, colorful kiddie table to eat ice cream and my favorite cake: angel food with confetti icing. Then I unwrapped presents in front of all of my classmates. Once, a girl named Jackie gave me a set of underwear with "Spank Me" embroidered on the bottom. I was mortified.

"She is never, ever, ever, ever, ever coming to my birthday party again," I shrieked to my mother later.

"If she's in your class next year, she's coming to your birthday party, or you're not having a birthday party at all," Mom said flatly.

Because I was so young, I only have a few memories of my father's junk business. But I vividly recall the place itself, which was roughly the size of a city block with mountains of rusted, twisted metal. George the Welder worked in a metal shop, and in the small office building was a mousy clerk named Job, and a rather large bookkeeper, Mrs. Butz—a name that cracked me up whenever I heard it.

The junkyard was a pretty simple operation. Customers hauled loads of salvaged scrap metal in a truck that was driven onto a giant scale embedded in the junkyard's driveway. The truck was weighed first, fully loaded, then again after it was emptied. The difference in the two weights determined the amount of scrap metal in the load. My father would pay his customers for their scrap and then resell it to third-party metal refiners.

Before anything got shipped off, however, Dad cherry-picked interesting old tools and other junk, saving them from the smelter. Junk is a relative word, of course, because many of the items in his collection were relics of early life on the frontier. It was mostly farm implements and hand tools—cast-iron tractor seats, grain grinders, saws, drills, hundreds of wrenches and hog oilers. (A hog oiler is basically a hollow metal ball that's filled with an ointment that keeps the bugs off a hog after it rubs up against it.) Dad's collection included some pretty unusual items, too, such as an old phonograph, an undertaker's embalming table, and even a rickety old Civil War-era cannon.

All of these items were heaped up in a metal shed—once a blacksmith's shop—and an old railroad boxcar. Unfortunately, some of the items were so rusty that they were unrecognizable. Those with moving parts had seized up over time. Over the years, my dad worked after hours and on weekends, painstakingly restoring each piece by hand, using wire brushes, steel wool, strippers, and solvents, as well as gallons of WD-40. Then, he identified and cataloged each piece, just waiting for the day he could display them for the world to see.

In his junkyard days, I once overheard my father telling Mom about a man and his wife who came in asking to use the scale. But it wasn't to weigh metal—it was to weigh the wife, who was both extremely stout and extremely pregnant. Apparently, her weight exceeded the capacity of the scale at the doctor's office, so the woman's physician sent her and her husband to Dad's junkyard scale. In an act of kindness, my father said he waited until the other customers had left the office before assisting the couple. The woman got into her husband's truck, and her husband drove it onto the scale to be weighed. Then she got out of the truck and stood on the sidewalk while the truck was weighed again without her. My father wrote her weight difference down on a piece of paper and handed it to the husband. I endlessly begged him to tell me how much the pregnant woman weighed, but he wouldn't spill the beans, not even to my mom.

On days Mom needed help watching us kids, she would drop us off at the junkyard and we would play in the heaps of scrap. It's a miracle that none of us ever severed or skewered a body part in all that sharp, rusty metal.

One clear memory of the junkyard sticks in my head. I was playing in the bookkeeper's office with Karan, surrounded by boxes of promotional calendars that my dad would be giving his customers for the New Year. Each calendar was branded Copeland Supply and featured a picture of a beautiful woman with movie-star hair. There were blondes, brunettes, and redheads, with a variety of hair-dos—beehives, buns, and braids. My sister and I would sift through the calendars to determine which women had the most beautiful hair-dos.

Those calendars came back to haunt me.

In school, we learned about how wheat becomes flour and later becomes bread. (An obvious subject, considering Kansas is dubbed "America's breadbasket.") As part of the lesson, our first-grade teacher took us on a field trip to the flour mill in town. At one point, my classmates and I—roughly 24 students in all—were clustered around the tour guide, who in exhaustive detail explained to us the entire milling process. It had that familiar sound I sometimes heard as a kid around adults: *Blah, blah, blah blah. Blah, blah blah. Blah, blah, blah.*

Bored and restless, I noticed one of my classmates raising his arm to point at something on the wall. I looked over and saw that he was pointing at one of my dad's calendars, with Copeland Supply in big, bold letters printed on the front. And for the first time—and I can't believe that I hadn't noticed this earlier—I realized that the woman on the calendar was topless! While I was looking at her movie-star hair, the rest of the world was looking at her bare breasts. All of a sudden, I was ashamed! Pointing at the calendar, my fellow classmate shouted, "Hey, Beth, isn't that your dad's place?" And like the Apostle Peter in his moment of cowardice, I adamantly denied any knowledge of Copeland Supply. In front of the whole class, I disavowed my dad.

"Nope, I've never heard of it."

4.
BETTY AND GOD

With a family of six, it became clear to my folks that it would take more than a junkyard to support us.

In 1972, an old-fashioned hardware store in downtown McPherson came up for sale. It was owned by an older couple named Lowell and Pauline Hawley, and they were ready to retire. Dad proposed buying Hawley Hardware for himself. But Mom said they could buy it only on one condition: She would own and run the store herself. My dad said she made it clear that there was no room for argument.

However, Mom faced one small problem: She didn't know a whit about hardware and had no real experience running a small business. But that didn't stop her. She had elbowed her way forward in the world ever since dropping out of school in the eighth grade. She knew how to make things happen.

In the few months leading up to the sale, Mom worked as a clerk at Hawley Hardware, with Lowell, Pauline, and three other clerks showing her the ropes. It was a big relief when the clerks agreed to stay on after the sale closed.

With the deal finalized, my parents moved everything inside Hawley Hardware to a building located two blocks north. The new business was named B&G Hardware after my parents, Betty and Gene. But not long after her store was up and running, Betty cut Gene out of the name entirely, telling people that B&G stood for "Betty and God."

The outside was unremarkable—it was a low-slung stucco building with a flat roof that caused endless headaches after every snowfall. Inside was a different story, pure nostalgia from wall-to-wall. The most memorable feature of B&G Hardware was the antique oak cabinetry that displayed the merchandise. Housewares and small appliances were arranged on bookcase-style shelves. Small, packaged tools hung from hooks on pegboards. Nails were raked from metal bins using a metal claw tool. Most impressive, however, were the items displayed in tall cases with glass doors and wooden drawers. Each item for sale was wired onto an orange felt panel behind the glass, and a label beneath it indicated the item's price and location within the cabinet. For example, a customer would point at a padlock, which had a label underneath that read $4.99 / 2F. The clerk opened the cabinet door to find the desired padlock inside Drawer 2 of Row F.

I was in the second grade when Mom entered the hardware business. Overnight, my life changed in both good and bad ways. Mom's store was open six days a week from 8 a.m. to 6 p.m., except on Thursdays, when it stayed open until 8:30 p.m. Suddenly, I lost my full-time Mom, the one who took me to tap-dance lessons, who made me a fish costume for a school play, who baked a cake or cookies almost every day—sometimes letting me lick the bowl.

Mom in the housewares department of B&G Hardware.

Because Mom was working, I was no longer able to go home for lunch, which seemed like a big deal at the time. My sister and I were among the few elementary school students who spent their lunch period in a musty classroom watched over by an old, cranky teacher—one who wouldn't allow us kids to move around or talk. Each morning, my mother packed us a sandwich—usually sliced turkey on buttered white bread—in a lunch box that looked like a barn, with a thermos that looked like a grain silo that couldn't keep our milk cold.

When I got to the store after school, I'd complain to my mother like I had a bad case of ringworm:

"Moooooommmmm, the milk in my silo is always warm."

I was too young to understand that Mom's business helped our family's finances. And it would take years for me to comprehend that my mother needed that store to fulfill her own sense of purpose. As a kid, I could see other moms attending my friends' school plays and softball games, and I wanted my mom to do the same. But she couldn't leave her store. After school, Ricky, Karan, and I were expected to walk or ride our bikes to Mom's store and stay there until closing. If Mom was busy, her customers often kept us kids in line, meaning that we had dozens of unofficial babysitters. Three of them were Loy, Arlene, and Gladys, Mom's part-time clerks.

In time, I grew curious about the wide variety of merchandise in Mom's store—bins and bins of bolts and screws, as well as an array of housewares, appliances, gifts, and power tools. I was starting to enjoy life in what had become my second home, the one filled with hardware. Ricky and I also became incredibly close, mainly because he was so funny. It stings a little, but there's nothing better than laughing so hard that milk comes out your nose. That happened a lot when I was with my brother.

In my final year of elementary school in 1974, the building next door to my mother's store on Main Street came up for sale. It, too, was a nondescript, low-slung stucco building. My father suggested that he and my mother take out a loan to purchase it, using my mother's store as collateral. The structure, a former auto dealership and repair shop, was much larger than his junkyard office, fueling my father's ambitions to expand.

Dad at the front counter of Copeland Supply.

Dad organized his store into three main sections. The front primarily carried hand tools, power tools, and painting supplies. It also had an auto parts counter on the side, with 20 or so shelving units carrying things like air filters, engine belts, distributor caps, and spark plugs. The middle part of the store was called the bolt room, and it held practically every type of fastener imaginable. Endless shelving units were divided into bins for the bolts, nuts, and washers. The bolt room also had a counter where freight and other deliveries were unpacked and priced before being shelved. (I found true love at the freight counter, but that came later.) The last section was in the very back of the building and held a metal-fabrication shop. Giant garage doors on each side of the steel shop were kept open in the summer and closed in the winter because the space didn't have air conditioning and heat.

Even though Mom and Dad carried much of the same merchandise, the stores were markedly different. Copeland Supply was both bigger and busier, serving mainly farmers, oilfield workers, and those with jobs in manufacturing. Dad's greatest gift, in my mind, was that he knew how to fix just about anything. When a customer faced a complicated repair or project, Dad would diagram the solution on the back of a paper sack, then fill it with the necessary parts or fittings the customer needed to buy.

Mom's store served mainly homeowners and hobbyists. The pace was slower, the mood set by elevator music on the local radio station. Customers were greeted individually with, "Can I help you?" and led to the merchandise. Next to the cash register was a candy case, where customers often lingered to buy a chocolate confection and chat.

Next to the cash register at Mom's store was a candy case,
where customers would often linger while enjoying a piece of chocolate.

My mom was beloved by her customers, mainly because she was such a good listener. It wasn't uncommon for someone with a leaky faucet, for example, to buy a 10-cent gasket, then stick around to visit a bit. As a result, Mom knew things like whose daughter was happily pregnant, or how much money was raised at the pancake supper, or who just bought a new house. At the same time, her customers trusted Mom's discretion enough to share deeply personal things as well—which is risky in a small town, where everybody knows everybody. God forbid there's a teen pregnancy, because word can travel fast. Of course, customers didn't expect Mom to fix their problems like they would a leaky faucet. They just wanted to say out loud the things that were weighing on their hearts—and to know that they weren't being judged. Mom's gift for compassion, I believe, sprang from tragedy in her own childhood that made her early years indescribably difficult.

Dad was as good at gabbing as Mom was at listening. To borrow one of his sayings, "He could talk the hide off a cow." Just about any piece of information that a customer shared somehow reminded Dad of a funny story from his days growing up on his family's farm or, later, from oilfield work across the Southwest. And all of his tales were delivered in his native East Texas drawl that somehow made them even funnier to his customers' Midwestern ears. For sure, the permanent frown on his face could be intimidating if you didn't know him. In fact, I once asked him why he never looked happy, and he said, "Bethy, if I smiled, nobody would recognize me."

Shortly after the stores were in business, Karan and I started noticing some peculiarities at home around the holidays. Before B&G Hardware existed, the Easter Bunny waited until we were asleep to leave a woven straw basket of candy at the foot of our beds. We used it to collect the hard-boiled eggs that were hidden in the house and around the backyard. After Mom got the store, the Easter Bunny left each of us a small, galvanized bucket, just like the ones stocked at her store.

Then at Christmas, Karan and I noticed that Santa's elves wrapped our presents in the exact same wrapping paper that Mom used for her customers' gifts. There were also consecutive years in which we would each receive a small plastic toolbox filled with DIY basics—screwdrivers, a rasp, a small saw, and a couple of wrenches. These all came from Dad's store. After Santa had left us a toolbox for the third or fourth year in a row, Karan and I just took them back to Dad's store and hung them on the display racks.

In the early days of the stores, Ricky, Karan, and I lollygagged around the two buildings after school and on Saturdays. Mom and Dad thought—rightly so—that if we were at home alone, we would get into trouble.

We started out by building forts out of cardboard boxes, wooden crates, and tarps. But it didn't take long for us to tire of our little shantytowns. Soon, our antics became more cutthroat. It was Ricky who usually dreamed them up. One game was a variation of hide-and-seek, and it took place in the bolt room of my dad's store. One person was declared "it" and given a little pouch full of roofing nails. While the other two of us hid behind shelving or somewhere else, "it" roamed up and down the aisles. When one of us was spotted, "it" hurled a big handful of roofing nails, which felt like a million little bee stings. You really had to crouch down and cover your eyes, just in case. The person who got assaulted with nails then became "it," taking over the nail pouch.

Another time, Ricky discovered a little door in an attic storage space. He jimmied the door open to reveal the concrete floor of the steel shop below us. Then, he called me and Karan up to the attic loft and dared us to jump down onto the shop floor. Karan immediately said "no" and left. Even to me, the thought of jumping onto a concrete floor felt a little too crazy. Obviously, Ricky hadn't seen the "Safety First" posters hanging in the steel shop. But my brother assured me that the distance *seemed* higher than it actually was. As I teetered on the edge of the loft, a little voice inside my head reminded me that Ricky had been reckless as long as I could remember. Once, he knocked out his front teeth after attempting to go down a slippery slide while standing up. Instead of gliding down on his feet, he pitched forward and landed face first on the pavement. I saw blood everywhere, along with pieces of his teeth. I refused to jump. Ricky called me a chicken, which made me so mad that I stomped off, just like Karan.

But a funny thing happened en route to the attic stairs. Something next to the handrail moved, catching my eye. When I got closer, I saw that it was a little wire hamster cage, with about a half-dozen mice running around inside. These were the same mice that my brother had been trapping in the Mason jars for money! Suddenly, I wasn't mad at Ricky anymore because the mice were alive after all. Then he explained his "system." Whenever he ran short on funds, he would take one of the mice out of the cage and put it in a Mason jar. He would show it to Dad, who gave him 25 cents. And just to be sure Dad wouldn't catch on to Ricky's double dipping, he rotated the mice through the Mason jars.

"It's easy money," my brother told me.

It's true that Ricky was always mischievous, but with his mischief came charm. He was always on the lookout for ways to rustle up some spending money or get something for free.

It started when Ricky figured out that a quarter-inch flat washer worked just as well as a penny in the gumball machine that Dad kept on the auto parts counter. Since the stores had a seemingly unlimited supply of flat washers, we could chew gum anytime we wanted. Still, free gum wasn't exactly the jackpot that Ricky was looking for. To bump up his take, Ricky once told me to run to the Gibson's store across the street, get an empty shopping cart, and roll it back to Dad's store.

Once he had the cart, Ricky rolled it over to the pop machine, next to which were wooden crates that held dozens of empty glass bottles. Together, we filled the shopping cart with empty bottles and rolled it back across the street to the customer-service counter at Gibson's. There, Ricky got the bottle-deposit money back in cash. Much later, I realized that Dad knew all along what we were doing, but he just shrugged it off. My father had to pay back the gumball-machine man for the flat washers, and the pop-machine man for the bottles.

It was time to tap into our energy and ingenuity and put us kids to work, my parents decided. It became my job to sweep the front of the store, and Karan restocked the paper goods—sacks, sales tickets, toilet paper, and bathroom hand towels. Ricky's job was to pick up in the steel shop and sweep the floors there after it closed at 5. By the end of the day, there would be a noticeable buildup of oil and dirt on the floor, and the oil got sticky if you didn't get rid of it. Dad had a big barrel of stuff called "floor sweep," which to me looked like cat litter. (In fact, Dad brought big bags of floor sweep home for use in Doorknob's litter box.) After applying a scoopful of floor sweep to each oil spot, the grease and dirt were swept up with a push broom and put in a trash bag that went in the dumpster.

The steel shop was humongous, which meant there was a lot of sweeping. So, Ricky figured out a way to make his job easier— and of course it involved me, his sidekick. First, I scooped floor sweep onto the oil spots while Ricky went to the bookkeeper's office at the front of the store. The "office gal," as Dad called her, had gone home for the day, so Ricky could "borrow" her desk chair, which was key because it had wheels on the bottom. He rolled the chair into the shop and sat down while holding the push broom. Ricky explained that my job was to push him all around the shop floor while he swept everything into a pile. Believe me, that chair was really hard to push with Ricky sitting in it. He was heavy, and the wheels got clogged with floor sweep. Making matters worse, the office chair also swiveled, and I couldn't roll Ricky in a straight line. Eventually, I had to stop because I was too tired to push my brother around anymore. And the shop floor looked just as dirty as it did when we started.

Seeing that I was totally pooped, Ricky scrapped the idea. He told me to keep sweeping while he returned the office chair. I waited and waited for him to relieve me but—and I should have known this all along—Ricky never came back, and I had to finish the job alone.

Ricky was just as impish on the home front. One Fourth of July, Ricky bought a bunch of Roman candles. Ricky gave me and a boy from the neighborhood two Roman candles each, and he kept two for himself. Next, he handed out metal trash can lids for us to use as shields. Pretending that we were the three cops in "The Mod Squad," we ran around a big field behind our house shooting balls of fire at each other. The game ended when the neighborhood kid's shirt sleeve caught on fire.

5.

NAME THAT BOLT

It's downright shocking to me how humble bolts and mere screws can come in so many variations. For starters, there are wood screws, sheet-metal screws, machine screws, and lag screws. The top of the screw, called the head, comes in multiple shapes, such as a flat head, round head, pan head, and hex head. Depending on the screwdriver used, the head can have a slotted groove, crossed grooves, or an opening for a hex key. The circumference of most screws is designated by a number, with a No. 6 screw being smaller around than a No. 16 screw, for example.

The bolt room at Copeland Supply was a labyrinth of fasteners.

Bolts also come in a variety of flavors. Both stores carried two main types: carriage bolts and hex head bolts. Some of these come in two finishes: rust-resistant galvanized (coated) or plain (uncoated). Adding "2" to the number of hash marks on a hex-head bolt determines the hardness of the metal. So, a bolt with no hash marks is a Grade 2 hardness, which is softer than a bolt with three hash marks (Grade 5) or six hash marks (Grade 8). There are also differences in bolts' thread counts, meaning the number of grooves on the shank. A "course" bolt has fewer threads per inch than a "fine" bolt. And unlike screws, the circumference of a bolt is measured in fractional inches, such as 1/4-inch, 5/16-inch, and 3/8-inch. Nuts and washers also come in a dizzying array of sizes and types, depending on their use.

It took time, but eventually I became so familiar with bolts and screws that I could usually identify their type, length, diameter, head style, and hardness just by looking at them. The secret: "Name That Bolt," a game Ricky invented. My brother would hold up a bolt or screw—the more obscure the better—and I would guess:

"Ummm, number 14 by four, slotted, flat-head wood screw?"

"Wrong! It's a number 12," he would say. "Here's one for Karan."

"Five-sixteenths by 2, grade-five, national fine, hex head cap screw?" she would say.

"Correct!"

The more we tried to stump each other, the better we got at the guessing game. As expected, Ricky usually won the most points in "Name That Bolt," even when I slipped in an occasional metric bolt, which is measured in millimeters. It's a good thing I didn't play for money.

Hardware is more than just fasteners, of course. To me, it seemed that everything my parents stocked—rope, drill bits, saw blades, wrenches, files, hinges, nails, gloves, pipe fittings, power drills, and shovels—came in a multitude of variations. It didn't make sense to me that 10-gauge wire is *bigger around* than 14-

gauge wire, while a No. 10 screw is *smaller around* than a No. 14. I had a lot to learn.

In this new role, I quickly realized that there were three main components to selling hardware. First, just finding what the customer needed was 50% of the job. And only by working at the stores day after day was I eventually able to locate most of the merchandise.

The next 30% of the job was more difficult: Just because I knew where something was, I didn't necessarily know what it did. For example, I could cut a length of copper tubing using a special tool that severed the soft metal without denting it. But customers who bought copper tubing also typically wanted copper ferrules, a little sleeve that slips over the tubing to create a tight seal with the fittings. In the beginning when I sold ferrules, I said this little prayer to myself, *Please don't ask what a ferrule does, please don't ask what a ferrule does, please don't ask what a ferrule does.*

Once again, with time and training, I could explain why and how various things were used. If something really stumped me, I usually tracked down my dad.

Once, a completely frazzled-looking customer came in and said, "I need help figuring out these plans for a jungle gym set."

On the front counter, he spread out a two-page diagram with lots of arrows and circles. Next to the plans he spread out a smorgasbord of little fasteners. Naturally, I did the only logical thing possible. I got on the intercom and announced over the storewide speakers, "Cope, please come to the front counter."

Dad finished whatever he was doing and walked to the counter. He saw the diagram and didn't say a word. He picked up both pages and studied them, turning the pages over thinking there might be more instructions on the back. There were none. Finally, he spoke.

"These plans don't make any sense," he said. "The fasteners pictured on the diagram don't match the fasteners that are included in the kit."

The customer looked both annoyed and relieved.

"If you put the jungle gym together with these parts, your kids will be in slings and stitches," Dad continued.

Dad put the man's plans to the side and drew a new diagram from scratch on the back of a paper sack. Together they gathered up the fasteners indicated on Dad's plan so the customer would know each fastener's purpose. Then Dad wrote the store's phone number on the sack, just in case the customer had questions when he got home. I'm guessing these step-by-step instructions took Dad about 40 minutes to go through. I rang up the final sale, which totaled less than $10.

Similar scenarios played out when we were out and about. One of our favorite restaurants in town was a fried-chicken place called Sir Robert's, or Sir Bob's for short. It was owned by my parents' good friends, Bob and Lois, and if possible, they would seat us at our favorite booth. The entire time we were at the table, people would stop by to say "hi" on their way in or out the door. But many of them would dawdle so they could ask in-depth questions about certain tools or seek advice on how to tackle a project.

For example, once a man asked his family to wait in the car while he talked to my dad. Looking miserable, he complained of water seeping into his basement through both the walls and the floor. With a growing mold problem, he was at a loss as to what to do. Our food had just arrived, including my father's favorite dish—chicken livers with mashed potatoes and gravy.

While Dad's supper got cold, he talked the man through various options, such as vapor barriers and waterproofing. Then Dad took a paper napkin and diagrammed how French drains worked.

"Thanks, Cope," the man said. "I'll look into these first thing tomorrow."

None of these solutions would lead to sales at his store because they were typically handled by tradesmen. But that didn't matter to my father. Meanwhile, we were finished eating, and Dad was just digging into his chicken livers.

Dad's ability to truly help people touches on the final 20% of the job: dealing with customers. Although it was the smallest part of the equation, it could have the largest impact. Both of my parents taught me to treat all customers the same. Always be courteous and fair—it didn't matter if the customer talked funny or looked different than you did.

"Their money is just as good here as anyone else's," Dad told me.

Unlike the customers at Mom's store, which was slower paced, the customers at Dad's were typically either farmers in a hurry or workmen who were "on the clock," with bosses who needed them back on the job. There was no lollygagging at his store. When possible, the clerks would even double-team, with one locating the merchandise while another would write up the ticket to speed up the process.

But if a casual customer came in and didn't seem like he was in a hurry, my father might have a little fun with him.

Let's say a homeowner walked in asking for some caulk. Dad would ask about the nature of the project to determine whether the caulk needed to be waterproof or adhesive, for example. After picking the caulk, Dad trotted out this old chestnut.

Dad: *"Now that you have the caulk, you'll also need a hen-way. Do you have one?"*

Customer: *"A what?"*

Dad: *"A hen-way."*

Customer: *"What's a hen-way?"*

Dad: *"Oh, about 4 or 5 pounds."*

That's about when the coffee drinkers would stop eating peanuts to elbow each other and chuckle softly.

Aside from Dad's humor, his mantra was, "Kill them with kindness," even though he was known to blow his stack from time to time. When he got to yelling, we knew to stand back to avoid the fine mist of spittle. It mainly happened at home, like if Doorknob threw up on the carpet or when Ricky shot a hole in the picture window with a BB gun.

Like my dad, I sometimes found it hard to hold my tongue too.

Once, there was a man who had moved to McPherson from a big company in California to help manage a pharmaceutical plant in town. Since he had just bought a house, he needed a lot of basic things. The man came to Mom's store on a Thursday evening, when her business stayed open until 8:30 p.m.

Mom and I were the only ones there, and he read off a long list of the things that he needed: flatware, mixing bowls, a frying pan and saucepan, a spatula and mixing spoon, pot holders, a spoon rest, canisters, drinking glasses and coffee cups, a toaster, can opener, and tea kettle. . .

"It might be easier if you gave us the list, and we can check off the items as we go along," I suggested.

"I like doing it this way," he said.

So, Mom and I worked like rented mules to gather up everything that this man asked for. And he was snappish if he had to repeat himself.

I don't remember the total of his bill, but it was big. Very big. In fact, the man bought so much stuff, the paper sacks we kept under the counter were too small to hold his mountain of purchases. So, Mom asked me to run out to her car and get some of the empty Dillons grocery sacks she kept in the trunk.

To the man, we must have looked like little termites as we scurried around. My mother asked me to help carry the sacks to the man's car and load them in his trunk.

Then he turned to Mom and said condescendingly, "That won't be necessary, I can manage just fine without your daughter."

I saw my mother stiffen. The tone of the man's voice when he spoke to Mom made me so angry, I was ready to tell the man where he could stuff those Dillons sacks. But before I could open my mouth, my mother subtly put her finger to her lips. *Let it go*, she was telling me.

Finally, after the customer left, I complained to my mother, "That man treated us like we're hayseeds!"

Maybe I was feeling the typical insecurities that some small-town folks feel when they're around urban—and urbane—people. But more than that, the customer talked down to us in a way I felt was wrong, no matter where he was from. But my mother wouldn't allow me to be sassy as payback.

Later that night, I heard Mom tell Dad what happened, especially the part where the customer treated us like serfs. Dad just shrugged and said, "I guess he thinks he shits cake," which made Mom laugh.

Although my parents treated their customers alike, they had radically different approaches to doing business. I had to remind myself of those distinctions every time I crossed the parking lot between the stores.

For one thing, my mom charged higher prices, even when the same thing could be purchased for less money from my dad. That embarrassed me sometimes, but Mom made it clear, saying, "Never apologize for the prices." Also, Mom didn't accept credit cards because she didn't want to pay any credit-card company fees. And only certain customers were allowed to open an in-house charge account, which lowered the risk of losing money when someone couldn't pay their bills.

At Dad's store, credit cards were gladly accepted, and pretty much any customer could open a charge account. On his checkout counter were three large Rolodex-style card holders. Each one was filled with plastic cards imprinted with the name, address, and account number of any person or business with a charge account. When a customer said "charge it," his plastic card was pulled, and an imprint was made in triplicate on the sales ticket. The customer took one copy as a receipt, the store kept the second copy for its records, and the bookkeeper filed the third copy in a manila folder so it could be mailed out with the monthly statements.

As I grew older, my parents felt I was ready for more responsibility. My big promotion from floor sweeping to salesclerk earned me a raise to $1.50 an hour, up from $1. I still remember my very first sale as a newly-minted clerk. My job was to stand at the checkout counter to write up sales tickets when the customers were ready to pay. Up walked one of my dad's regulars—a man named Red, who owned a ditch-digging service. Red set a roll of gray tape on the counter and said to me, "duct tape." On the sales ticket, I dutifully wrote "duck tape," because that's what duct sounds like when spoken. Red let out a big laugh.

Another time I asked a customer if he needed "*gla*vanized" bolts, mispronouncing "galvanized." That drew big guffaws from Arthur and his band of coffee drinkers who sat around shelling peanuts all day. They were literally my peanut gallery, but I was fond of them, nonetheless. Every time they called me Miss Nuisance, I just rolled my eyes.

Before retiring, Arthur worked as a mechanic for a major oilfield producer. Originally from Oklahoma, Arthur had been in a terrible car accident, which left one of his legs shorter than the other. Even with a special shoe, Arthur had a pronounced limp, and he grimaced slightly when he walked. But none of that mattered to me. Arthur would notice if I had the sniffles. Arthur smiled at my jokes. Arthur clipped out articles from *Newsweek* that he thought I might find interesting. It was Arthur who nicknamed me Miss Nuisance, and I had become an amusing source of entertainment to him and the other coffee drinkers.

Overall, I had grown pretty comfortable working at both of my parents' stores. But no matter how comfortable I got, I never stopped dreading Christmas.

December was my mother's peak selling season. In fact, she called it her "make or break" month, meaning those 31 days decided whether her business would turn a profit that year. Mom's store stayed open until 8:30 p.m. six days a week, and from 1 to 5 p.m. on Sundays. It upended our lives both at the store and at home.

"If you need me, you can find me at the store," Mom told everyone. When the holiday rush was at full tilt, Dad would help out at Mom's after he closed his own store for the day.

But mainly, I disliked Christmas because at Mom's store, gift-wrapping was free. After school and on the weekends, I got stuck in a small, drab room with a concrete floor and a single light fixture: the wrapping room. It was my personal jail cell throughout the holidays. Each day, I would work my way through a pile of purchases that customers had left behind. They were wrapped in red and white paper and topped with anemic-looking bows that Mom made with 13 turns on a hand-cranked bow-making machine. I once suggested that she make more robust bows with 20 cranks on the machine, but she didn't want to run out of ribbon. At closing time, I loaded the gifts into the back seat of Mom's car, and she drove me around town to deliver them to customers' houses. Unless the gift was a surprise, I ran the gift up to the front porch and rang the doorbell. If the gift was a secret, Mom pre-arranged to have me leave it on the back porch so it could be picked up and hidden.

My days were long, and occasionally I reminded my mother of America's child-labor laws. She pretended not to hear me.

By the time Christmas Eve rolled around, we were all too exhausted to go to church. The next day, Christmas morning, we opened up a lot of envelopes with gift certificates inside because my parents were so busy, there was no time for them to go Christmas shopping.

On one hand, I could use the gift certificates to choose the clothes and other things I wanted. But on the other, it was hard going back to school after Christmas break and seeing all of the cool things my friends' parents surprised them with.

Free gift-wrapping was just one part of what Mom called her "winning strategy." And her words weren't just idle talk. A Kmart had recently opened in town, and it was selling some of the same household goods as my mother, but at lower prices.

"Customer service is what sets me apart from Kmart and the

other big stores," she said. "The competition can't offer things like gift wrapping, bridal registries, and home delivery." To her, customer service started the moment someone walked in the front door and was greeted with, "Can I help you?"

Being the daughter of the stores' owners gave me a fair amount of job security. Luckily that worked in my favor after I made my biggest mistake ever. The incident will be forever known as "The Day Bethy Lost the Bank Bag."

One morning, my mother put all the cash and checks collected the previous day into the zippered bank bag and asked me to make a deposit. Using bungee cords, I strapped the bag to a rack on the back of my bicycle. Then I rode down the alley between my parents' stores and the bank. When I arrived, I got off my bike—and the bag was gone! The bungee cords were just hanging from my bike rack. Somewhere along the way, the bag must have fallen off. I frantically searched the bank parking lot and rode up and down the alley in hopes of seeing it on the ground. But, no, the bank bag was gone.

When I returned to my mom's store, I was blubbering so much that she couldn't understand what I was saying. Eventually, I was able to choke out that I had lost the bank bag. Mom called Dad, and together they retraced my route along the alley between the stores and the bank. But the bag was nowhere to be found. An entire day's worth of business was lost. Mom didn't punish me—even though I totally deserved it.

But there was another, larger reason for my anguish. I remember that when I came back from the bank in tears and blubbering, my mother couldn't understand the first few sentences out of my mouth. But what I was saying was this: "I'm not like Ricky. I swear, I'm not like Ricky." My brother was becoming more devious, and I wanted her to know that I hadn't taken the money from the bank bag.

My mom took a big financial hit that day, and the guilt affects me even now. But there was a small measure of redemption. The following month, my mother's customers started coming back to her store to say that their checks hadn't cleared. Each one was told, "Bethy lost the bank bag."

And each one wrote a new check to my mother.

That's how small towns work: People look out for each other. Many of our customers were likely the same people we went to church with. Or they were the parents of my friends at school. Or they belonged to the same clubs or fraternal organizations. That tight-knit sense of community can be such a blessing. But it can also lead to awkward encounters.

My dad was proud to be a member of a Masonic lodge, even though some people in town believed that Masonic secrets and rituals were evil. Once, a deacon from our church told Dad that he could be a Mason or he could be a Baptist, but he couldn't be both. The deacon then said he'd come back the following week for Dad's decision.

"I don't need a week," Dad said. "I can give you my answer right now."

"So, which will it be?" the deacon asked.

"I'm not going to quit either one, and that's that," Dad told him.

The matter never came back up again as far as I know, and Dad continued to be both a Mason and a Baptist.

He also attended night school at one of the two small, liberal arts colleges in town. McPherson College offered the most variety, and he took whatever classes were available in the evenings–astronomy, geology, and religion. (Despite earning plenty of credits, he didn't have enough in a single discipline to earn a degree.) He was Scoutmaster when my brothers were in the Boy Scouts. He held membership cards to the V.F.W. and the American Legion because of his service in World War II and the Korean War.

As a kid, I thought Dad's civic activities were pretty boring. That is, except for one. Every year on the second Friday in May, McPherson holds its All Schools Day celebration. All of the little towns throughout the county come to McPherson to participate. It's called May Day for short and continues to this day. The highlight of May Day is a parade down Main Street that opens with a man dressed like Uncle Sam, followed by some soldiers carrying the American and Kansas flags. Then politicians—sometimes even the governor if it's an election year—ride in convertibles and wave at the thousands of people who come to town just for May Day. Various floats decorated with crepe paper and tissue flowers carry every kindergarten class in the county down Main Street. Older kids decorate their bikes and wear goofy costumes, forming a bicycle brigade to ride down Main. And every high school in the county elects a May Queen and a Prince Charming who wear glittering crowns and ride on thrones set atop individual floats.

Schools throughout the county bring marching bands, and some of them do fancy footwork while playing songs. And most—but not all—of the baton twirlers at the head of each band can throw their batons high in the air and catch them while marching in step.

As part of the Masons, Dad was also a Shriner, and he appeared in every May Day parade that I can remember as a kid. He wore a red-velvet fez and joined his fellow Shriners as they drove miniature Model-T cars down Main Street. My dad's fez was special because it had "Camel Herder" spelled out across the front in little rhinestones. He earned that designation after recruiting other men to join the club. In the weeks leading up to May Day, Dad and other Shriners with mini-Model-Ts met up at the high school parking lot to practice making zig-zags and crazy-eights with their cars. Afterward, they would hang out for a while—and Dad would come home a little woozy. When I got older, I realized that they were "practicing" just so they could pop open some beers and shoot the breeze.

Because of Dad's size—over six feet tall and roughly 220 pounds—he had to squeeze his body into his miniature car. The parade route was six or seven blocks long, and toward the end, Dad's Model-T would invariably get a flat tire because of his weight. As a solution, one of the Shriners bought a miniature tow truck. When Dad got the flat tire, the little tow truck would hook up Dad's Model T and pull it to the end of the route. It happened so often that people just assumed it was part of the act.

For McPherson's annual All Schools Day parade, Dad donned his Shriner's fez and drove a mini-Model T down Main Street.

On the day of the parade, Mom would bring in a Crock-Pot full of baked beans and a roaster with pulled pork to her store. She set it out on a card table, along with potato salad and coleslaw from Dillons. She kept a cake and some brownies in the office, reserving them for family and special friends. A lot of people came to fix themselves a plate, but they didn't stick around to buy anything. The truth is, my parents didn't do much business on the day of the parade. Main Street was closed to traffic for the whole morning, so it was hard to even get to their stores. But the main reason was that the holding area for the horses was in front of Dad's building. By the time they got the go-ahead to march down Main, the street was covered with big clods of manure. Until the street sweeper came by, the air was so smelly and thick with flies that nobody wanted to park in front of the stores.

The parade was the highlight, but most of my friends agreed

that the best part of May Day was the carnival that came to town. Ricky was really good at the games—things like throwing darts at balloons or tossing a dime into a glass. One year he won two velvety fabric snakes and gave them to me and Karan. We hung them over the posts of our canopy beds.

The carnival featured amusement park rides, games with prizes, and of course, cotton candy and corn dogs. Only once did I go on the carnival's scariest ride: The Zipper. In talking me into getting on the ride, my brother Ricky tried to make it sound fun.

"The Zipper basically spins you around and upside down until you can actually taste the corn dog in the back of your throat."

One time, Karan and I were at the May Day carnival when it started to rain. *The sun is out,* I thought. *How can it be raining?* Then I realized: *This isn't rain!*

We were standing next to a ride called "The Spider," and some boys from Karan's class were on it. Every time their car twirled past us, they spit at us! Once we figured that out, Karan started screaming at them, which somehow made *us* look bad, not the boys. I had to take my sister by the arm and pull her away from the scene.

Karan was struggling. My sister's mood swings were affecting her at school, both academically and behaviorally. I could see it for myself. When I was in middle school, my fifth-grade teacher was leading me and my classmates single file down a staircase to take us to recess. As we passed Karan's classroom on the way down, I saw that her sixth-grade teacher had drawn a chalk circle on the classroom door. And there was my sister, standing against the door with her nose in the center of the circle as punishment. My classmates were laughing at her while she peered at us out of the corner of her eye. I was conflicted. I felt bad for Karan because everybody was laughing at her. But I was also embarrassed because that girl with her nose in the circle was my sister.

Maybe the problem wasn't Karan. Maybe the problem was us. We considered my sister difficult, when in fact maybe she was just different. True, she was moody. She sometimes had a terrible temper and was easily frustrated. But there was another side that people overlooked. Early on Karan showed an interest in classical music, when the rest of us liked rock or country or whatever top hits were playing on the radio. She stayed up late into the night listening to *Mystery Theater* on the radio, head buried under her covers. So, it was hard for her to get up in the mornings and get ready for school. Her spiral notebooks were full of free-form verse and poetry, including one titled, "To Cream the Ass of a Bitch." On top of it all, undiagnosed dyslexia and mental-health issues made learning difficult and frustrating.

As a result, she hung out with friends who were outcasts like herself. They didn't do well in school, stayed out late, and likely experimented with beer and cigarettes.

Small towns like McPherson are great at fostering a sense of community. But sometimes they aren't so great at accepting people who stick out or, worse, have behavioral issues.

In McPherson, one place where people *had* to be nice to Karan was church. My entire family went to the Baptist church every week when I was young. I wasn't particularly fond of the worship service, which included a windy sermon with a familiar refrain: *"Blah, blah, blah, blah, blah."* In my mind, the service was enjoyable only once a month on communion Sunday, when the kids could wait by the kitchen door after the service was over and take home the leftover bread and grape juice.

I loved Sunday School, however, especially when Bible stories were acted out with felt puppets—Jesus and the disciples, Jonah and the whale, Zacchaeus and the tree. There were crafts galore, with projects like a paper mâché nativity scene and fish symbols formed with beads. Each week, my friend's mom stopped by our classroom to play the guitar while we sang with gusto "Give Me Oil in My Lamp," "Deep and Wide," and, of course, "Jesus Loves Me."

In my early years, most of the Bible lessons I learned shared common themes: be nice to others, don't lie, be humble, respect your elders. These basics made it pretty easy to be a Christian. I mean, a person doesn't have to be particularly religious to embrace the fundamentals. In fact, as a kid, it was a comfort to me that someone knew all the answers when I didn't even know the questions.

My father taught Sunday School in a class for the oldest adults in the congregation, and my mother often made brownies for him to take. Mom was a big believer in "God is love." But a close second was, "Food is love." Before she got too busy with her hardware store, she baked mountains of cookies for Vacation Bible School and brought giant pots of chili to youth gatherings. She helped out at potluck dinners and served punch at wedding receptions in Fellowship Hall. When someone went into the hospital—it didn't have to be a fellow churchgoer—she would stop by to deliver a milkshake to the patient. Somehow, all of this was done in her low-key way. The last thing Mom ever wanted was to be the center of attention.

Out of all the Copeland children, Ronnie was easily the most religious and deeply involved in church activities. He and other members of "Sonshine," the youth choir, frequently performed at places like nursing homes and senior centers.

As for me, I was happy when I was at church. I could see my friends, and there were lots of fun activities. Only now do I realize that I didn't entirely grasp what it meant to be a believer. The first time I saw *The Flying Nun* on TV, I told Karan that I wanted to be a nun, just like Sally Field. Then, my sister informed me that to be a nun, I would have to get spayed, like the neighbor's dog was. That came as a complete surprise to me, and my enthusiasm to join a convent faded.

When you grow up going to church, you're basically with the same kids year after year. You get to know them in a deeper way than if you only see them at school.

One of my friends was incredibly pious, and when she was

moved by the spirit, she would shout, "Amen." That's not terribly unusual in a Baptist church. She was even more noticeable when she prayed. She would hold one hand in the air and swivel her palm in a Queen of England sort of way. Eyes closed, hand waving, she would say over and over, "YES, Jesus. THANK YOU, Jesus," throughout the prayer. I didn't laugh, because I could see that she was being sincere.

She's the one who taught me that if anyone ever asked, "What's your sign?" there could be only one correct answer. It wasn't Taurus or Gemini or some other Zodiac symbol. No, if someone were to ask, "What's your sign?" the correct answer was: "The cross."

A big milestone in a person's faith journey is the day you're baptized. Baptists practice full immersion, and it can only happen when followers are old enough to understand their commitment to the faith. For me, that was age 13, which coincidentally was the most physically awkward and emotionally insecure stage of my life.

On the morning of the ceremony, a large tank behind the choir loft was filled with warm water, which in my opinion beat being dunked in the Jordan River like Jesus was. I was told to bring one of my dad's handkerchiefs, which the pastor would use to wipe off my face after I came up from the water. Before the service started, I changed into a white robe and waited with a few other baptizees at the top of the steps that led into the tank. When it was my turn to descend, I walked down the steps, but I forgot to hold my dad's handkerchief up in the air and instead dragged it through the water. When I handed my hankie to the pastor, it was soaked. The pastor said some words, and I affirmed my faith. Then he put his arm around my shoulders and dipped me backwards into the water. I was nervous about my head going under, afraid that water would go up my nose and I would come up choking. I didn't want to look like a heathen, gagging in front of the whole congregation.

That didn't happen. But what did happen was worse. When I

came up from the water, the pastor couldn't dry my face using a wet hankie, so I used my hands to wipe my eyes. That's when I looked down and saw that my white robe was tightly clinging to my skin—and I could see my underpants through the fabric. Since that's all I was wearing under my robe, I was certain that everyone in the congregation could see my boobs! That would have been traumatic for anyone, of course, but the 13-year-old me was self-conscious about her body. I was horrified. I practically ran up the steps to get out of the tank, and I scurried to the bathroom to change into dry clothes.

After I blow-dried my hair, I returned to the sanctuary to join my parents in their pew.

"Could you see my boobs?" I whispered in a panic.

"You might want to keep your voice down," my father responded.

Still, I asked again, this time trying to be quieter. "Mom, could you see my boobs?"

"Bethy, you were too far away from the pews for anyone to see your boobs. Really and truly, you looked fine," my mother said reassuringly.

Nonetheless, I practically ran to the car when the last syllable of the benediction was spoken.

My religious education was supposed to instill in me a basic sense of morals and ethics that I would carry throughout my lifetime. But my spiritual development was very much a work in progress. Growing up, I tried hard to be my very best self, but sometimes I struggled—especially when I was around my sister. Karan endured a lot of teasing from me and Ricky, as well as the kids at school, especially because she was overweight. Being chubby myself, I should have been more sensitive to Karan's feelings. But I wasn't. In one of Karan's many attempts to drop some pounds, she cut back on salt, telling me that her weight was primarily due to water retention. I snorted back, "What exactly are you retaining? Hoover Dam?" Maybe too much of Ricky's smart-mouth personality had rubbed off on me. True, I didn't have his sneaky traits and schemes. But I often suffered lapses in kindness and goodwill.

One of my schoolteachers gently conveyed that message to me in my end-of-year report card. I got decent grades in various subjects, but my work habits—things like attentiveness and time management—were checked-marked "Needs Improvement." Like Ricky, I could get bored easily. In a separate note, the teacher complimented me on my sense of humor, which made me feel good. But it closed with this: "Just remember the joy you can add to people's lives with a smile and a kind word." It made me stop and think a bit.

6.
STRIVING FOR PROSPERITY

My parents had a Golden Rule: If someone does business with you, then you do business with them. So, if our last car came from the Ford dealership, the next car came from the Dodge dealership. Same with TVs and furniture, purchased from storefronts along Main Street that boasted four lanes of traffic and a meter maid who ticketed anyone who exceeded the time limit on their parking space.

In the early to mid-1970s, almost all of the storefronts in McPherson's core business district were occupied. At that time, there was enough business in downtown McPherson to support at least two stores that carried similar merchandise: two furniture stores, two jewelers, two drugstores, and even two five-and-dimes—Duckwall's and a Woolworth store. The latter had a lunch counter that served delicious grilled cheese sandwiches and other fast fare. Multiple clothing stores featured everything from the latest trends for young people to formal suits and dresses for their parents. There were three banks downtown, including one that once hosted a Space Age exhibit featuring a piece of moon rock under glass, guarded by a man in uniform.

Beyond Main Street, there were a number of grocery stores. My favorite was the Dillons store close to my house because it issued a "Cookie Card" to the customers' children. Every time Mom shopped for groceries there, I showed my personalized card at the bakery counter to get a cookie so large that it took two hands to hold it.

McPherson also had two movie theaters, which seems unusual considering how small the town was. It had a regular sit-down movie theater downtown, and a drive-in on the edge of town with a giant screen and little speakers that you mounted on your car windows.

Once, I begged Mom to take me to the drive-in theater to see a movie called *Tommy*, because at the time we had an orange tabby cat named Tommy. Somehow, I must have thought the film would be about my cat. But there were no cats whatsoever. Instead, one scene showed baked beans coming out of a TV set onto white carpet. In another scene, Tommy got into an "iron maiden" studded with syringes. That's about the point where Mom started the car in a huff and we drove home.

Family finances never came up at home—my folks didn't want us kids to worry about money. At my age, I had no way to discern whether business was "good" or "bad." When head-scratchers like this emerged, I often turned to my older brother. Once, Ronnie called me into his room when my favorite song came on the radio: "Tie a Yellow Ribbon Round the Ole Oak Tree." As the tune played, I lay on the bed watching my brother do his math homework. In his hand was a high-tech gadget that had recently come on the market: a calculator capable of doing advanced functions, such as trigonometry and exponentials. It was far more sophisticated than the adding machines that we used at the stores. Ronnie paid over $100 for his calculator, a considerable sum at the time. But he explained that it was a "good investment" that would help him when he went to college.

Watching my brother must have turned my thoughts to money. "Is our family rich?" I asked.

"Why on earth would you think that?" he said.

"Because we own two stores," I said.

Without hesitating, Ronnie said, "Just because we own the stores doesn't mean we're rich. Think about all of the stuff they carry," he explained. "What we own are stores full of merchandise that has to be paid for in advance with the hopes that people buy enough for us to make a profit. What money we have is tied up in inventory."

Who knew? I had just assumed that two stores meant we were rolling in dough. In fact, I boasted about it the summer before at Camp Washunga, where I joined other Baptist youth from across the state for a week to sing "Kumbaya" and make God's Eyes from yarn. One night, we were sitting around a campfire as someone strummed "Pass It On" softly on the guitar. Based on previous experience, I knew that at any second, someone would stand up and announce, "I am ready to turn my life over to Jesus Christ, my lord and savior." Meanwhile, I was flirting with a cute boy from Topeka. Oblivious to spiritual awakenings, the boy asked me, "What do your parents do?" Stretching the truth, I replied, "They own a *chain* of hardware stores." Happily, I didn't have to explain that the "chain" only had two links.

While I was beginning to understand the economics of owning a business, I was pretty clueless about the world around me. Nixon's Watergate scandal dominated newspaper headlines and the 10 o'clock news, but the brouhaha was a mystery to me. I finally said to my mother, "Watergate! Watergate! Watergate! That's all I hear about anymore. What is Watergate?"

My mother replied, "It's a hotel."

Then I was even more confused.

One global event was impossible to ignore. In 1973, the Organization of the Petroleum Exporting Countries (OPEC) embargoed shipments of crude oil to the U.S. As a result, energy prices skyrocketed, leading to fuel shortages and long lines at gas stations. Higher prices affected everyone, but farmers who came into my father's store talked about significant expenses just to keep their machinery moving.

"I paid purt near $50 to fill up my tractor," one customer complained to me as I wrote up his sales ticket.

The sluggish farm economy, in turn, led to falling sales at the hardware stores. Customers continued to buy the things they needed for repairs and to keep their equipment and operations running smoothly. But discretionary purchases, such as new appliances, lawnmowers, and barbecue grills, were slipping.

Still, the turmoil in the world around me had little impact on my day-to-day life. In fact, I was humming along at school with decent grades—even in math, my weakest subject. And because I worked at my parents' stores, I earned enough money to buy into two big trends: preppy clothing and a "mood ring," which purportedly changed colors based on my frame of mind. My goal was to earn a spot in the coveted place among "the popular girls." To help my cause, I joined a softball team, I was learning to play the clarinet in band class, and I won an essay contest themed, "I'm Proud to Be an American."

I inadvertently got my first clue that world events were putting a dent in our family's finances one Sunday morning in the depths of winter. I was wearing a new pair of shoes that my mother bought for me the day before. They were beautiful—a cream-colored leather, with a brown suede detail stitched on each side. I couldn't wait to wow my friends at school the next day.

On that frigid morning, Ricky and I walked to Lakeside Park, which was only a few blocks from our home via a shortcut along the railroad tracks. We arrived at the park to find the lake completely frozen over. We threw rocks onto the sheet of ice that covered the surface, and they bounced off or skittered away. That emboldened my brother, who convinced me that we could walk across the ice to the other side of the lake.

Because I was smaller and lighter, Ricky decided that I should take the first steps onto the ice. My brother held onto one of my hands as I leaned over the edge of the lake. I put my right foot onto the ice, and it held. Then I let go of my brother's hand so I could put my other foot on the ice. And at that moment, my right foot broke through the ice and plunged into the frigid water. Ricky was able to grab my arm and yank me back, but in pulling my foot out of the pond, my beautiful new shoe came off my foot, and it sank into the murky water. It was too far out and too deep to retrieve, but at least I was safe. At that point, my biggest concern was walking home in freezing temperatures wearing only a sopping wet sock on my right foot. Ricky had me take off the sock, and he gave me both of his socks to put on my bare foot, making the walk home a little less miserable. *Wow, he's looking out for me,* I thought. First, he saved me from falling into the lake, then he saved my foot from frostbite. He was basically a schemer, but he had a big heart.

When we got home, my mother was in the kitchen. "What happened? Where is your shoe?" she asked me.

"It sank into the pond at Lakeside Park when we tried to walk across the ice," I explained. I waited for her to express relief that I had come to no harm.

"I guess you now expect me to buy you another new pair of shoes?" she said.

"Yes?" I replied, tentatively.

"Well, no. You'll have to wait," was her answer.

For the first time, I realized how my two worlds were connected—that what happened at the stores affected what happened at home. I began to notice other ways my folks were finding to economize. Despite my bitter complaints, I wore hand-me-down clothes because to my mother, they were perfectly good and perfectly free. When we wanted pizza, we ate the frozen kind instead of getting one delivered from Pizza Hut. We dried our hands on terry-cloth towels rather than paper towels, which just ended up in the trash.

Economics was a big reason my mother put so much effort into promoting her store. My father could count on having a steady stream of customers at his store because it sold industrial supplies to farmers, manufacturers, oilfield workers, and other businesses that relied on him when something broke down. Conversely, my mother's store drew in more casual shoppers, many of whom were making discretionary purchases. As a result, Mom needed to heavily promote her business to create a steady flow of customers.

Every spring, she ordered big boxes of B&G Hardware-branded sales fliers that featured discounted merchandise, along with a coupon for a free screwdriver. Her plan was to have the family throw the fliers into everyone's front yard.

"You could just have the fliers inserted in the *McPherson Sentinel*," Dad suggested. "It would be a lot less trouble."

"But that would cost money," Mom said. "If we do it ourselves, the job gets done for free," she said.

Then Ricky chimed in, mimicking John Belushi on *Saturday Night Live.*

"We could just have the fliers inserted in the *McPherson Sentinel*. But noooooooooooooo!"

For roughly one week, Mom enlisted Ricky, Karan, and me to help with the fliers. After supper each night, we took our seats in the family room behind a tall stack of newspaper fliers and a pile of rubber bands. Over and over for what seemed like a million times, we rolled up fliers, rubber-banded them, and threw them on the floor. By the end of the night, the three of us were knee-deep in newspaper fliers. These were scooped up and stuffed into Dillons sacks that were then lined up in the living room. After five or six nights of this, the living room floor was covered wall-to-wall in grocery bags with only a small aisle to the front door.

For the next four Sundays, Dad backed his pickup into the driveway so we could load the truck bed with two beanbag chairs—one on each side—and roughly 20 sacks of fliers. Loading any more than that, we discovered, the fliers would blow out of the truck bed. Then, while Mom drove the truck up and down the streets of McPherson, two of us kids sat on the beanbag chairs, throwing fliers into everyone's front yard. Since there were three of us for a two-person job, Karan, Ricky, and I rotated our "shifts" on the beanbag chairs. But after a couple of Sundays of throwing duty, Ricky and Karan abandoned their posts. They hung out with a rougher crowd by then and said they had better use of their time than throwing fliers from the back of a truck.

As a result, Dad had to take over one of the bean bag chairs with me in the other one.

Uh-oh, I thought to myself. *I know what's coming.*

Dad was legendary in our family for hair-trigger carsickness. He insisted on driving everywhere because just sitting in the passenger seat while backing out of the driveway could nauseate him.

Mom drove the truck up and down the streets, and since it was a Sunday, lots of kids were out playing in their front yards. I was throwing flier after flier from my side of the truck. Behind me, I could hear Dad's play-by-play commentary.

"I'm developing a light film of sweat on my upper lip now!" he cried out.

Then, a few blocks later, the monologue continued. "Burrrrrrp! I'm separating the gases from the juices now!"

Not long after, he said in a low, halting voice, "My innards are. . .starting. . .to. . .churn. . .now."

Finally, he hollered, "BETTY! PULL. OVER. NOW!"

Mom came to a dead halt on North High Drive. I turned and saw my dad on his beanbag chair, hanging his head over the side of the pickup. When the children heard his loud retching, they all stopped what they were doing to watch. Soon, Dad was standing up in the bed of the truck and puking right in the middle of the street. I remember asking God at that very moment to open up the Earth so it could swallow me whole. Finally, Dad finished hurling. Mom started up the truck and drove home very slowly.

Once we pulled into the driveway, Mom helped Dad get out of the truck bed and led him to their bedroom to lie down. Meanwhile, I hosed down what looked like a vomit waterfall on the side of the truck. When I finished, Mom had me take my place on a beanbag chair.

"You're going solo," she said.

Mom drove down each street twice so I could throw fliers at homes on both sides of the road. After a while, I complained that my arm was ready to fall off, so she treated me to my favorite burrito at Taco Tico. On the drive home, I sat on my beanbag in the back of the truck and ate my reward for a job well done. For the next two Sundays, Dad diligently took some Dramamine long before taking his place on the beanbag chair.

Ricky and Karan were withdrawing from our family life in other ways. They both dropped out of church, refusing to go, even when my parents insisted. Then Mom and Dad stopped attending. They were still firm believers and knew that they had been "saved." But the stores consumed an incredible amount of their time and energy, and raising unruly kids was another full-time job. Sunday was their only day off, and they wanted to rest. I didn't think skipping church made them sinful because, hey, even God took a break on the seventh day.

I continued going to Sunday School. It was more fun than the church service because the lessons were more engaging. Except perhaps the one devoted to the evils of masturbation. The teacher read the scripture and explained that masturbation was a form of sexual intercourse, which was only permitted after a God-sanctioned marriage. My classmates and I were barely past puberty at that point, and just the thought of sex was still a source of embarrassment. Along with the rest of my friends, I had my eyes firmly fixed on the floor, jaw clenched. I left the lesson certain that I was a terrible sinner, doomed to the pits of hell into perpetuity.

I was starting to feel like my faith was lagging compared to others, even though I strongly believed in God (and still do). Not helping matters was a stop in the local Christian Book Store I made with one of my classmates. We were just browsing the displays when I pulled a Bible from a shelf. When I started to open the cover, I spotted a giant spider on the edge of the book. Frightened, I shrieked loudly and threw the Bible on the floor, like it had burned my hand. Since nobody else in the store saw the spider, it was obvious to them that I was possessed by Satan. At that moment, I was sure that my friend would encourage me to visit a member of our church who was known to perform ritual exorcisms.

Of course, now I realize that I was suffering typical adolescent insecurities. Still, I was terrible in athletics, not once earning a presidential patch in physical fitness that the cool kids had sewn all over their gym uniforms. My looks did nothing to help my cause— I was chubby and wore thick glasses to correct my double vision. And all the Jell-O that my mother made to help me lose weight had no effect on how I was feeling. And I wasn't the only one who didn't fit in. It felt like everyone in my family was weird (except for Ronnie). In short, my family was loud and quirky, and we stuck out wherever we went.

One of my mother's favorite activities was going to the movies, which for whatever reason she still called the "picture show," like we were all living in the 1930s. I loved the movies, too, but Mom embarrassed me whenever we went to the sit-down theater. That's because any time printed words appeared on the screen, Mom would read them aloud. Just imagine: We'd be sitting in the darkened theater with gobs of other people around us. Then, all of a sudden, my mom would cry out, "TWO WEEKS LATER," or "LOS ANGELES, CALIFORNIA," when the words appeared on the screen. Another annoying habit: Mom would loudly ask questions that couldn't be answered yet. For example, the movie had a scene where the lights went out, then you heard a gunshot. When the lights came back on, a dead person would be lying on the floor. That's when Mom would exclaim, "WHO DID THAT?" All of the people sitting in front of us would turn and shush us.

Epitomizing my embarrassment was the time the muffler fell off my mother's Pontiac, making a deafening rumble as she drove around town. When Mom dropped me off in front of my school, everyone turned and gawked when her car roared up to the curb. Making matters worse, my father's temporary solution was to reattach the muffler to the bottom of the car using a wire coat hanger.

To stifle my insecurity, I immersed myself in the stores. Being there was far more fun than being at school. I wore a work shirt with my name on it and carried a tape measure and pocketknife. I heard lots of interesting stories from customers who had lost their fingers. And I earned money to buy James Taylor albums. And perhaps more important, as I ran back and forth between the parking lot that separated the stores, I was beginning to evolve (mostly anyway) into my better self.

My mother's most popular—and my favorite—annual marketing campaign was the "Summer Sales Bonanza," which was held on a Saturday in July. The atmosphere felt like a circus—just with hardware instead of elephants.

One of Mom's wholesale hardware suppliers provided a giant banner that was hung across the front of her building. The supplier also threw in two big boxes of wooden yardsticks branded with "B&G Hardware."

On the day of the bonanza, everyone had a specific job. Just before Mom's store opened at 8 a.m., we took our posts.

Dad manned a barbecue grill in the parking lot and cooked up hot dogs. Next to him was a soda dispenser, and it was my duty to hand out cold pop in paper cups. (Happily, the dispenser included Mountain Dew, my favorite, and I liberally took advantage of my position throughout the day.) Soon, the parking lot was abuzz with people. In our maiden event, unfortunately, there were a few hiccups. First, the customers at Dad's store lined up for the free hot dogs, making it difficult for Mom's customers to get one. By mid-morning, Dad had to run to the supermarket for more wieners and buns.

"It's a wurst-case scenario," my father quipped.

Nearby, Ricky set up a grungy old car hood on sawhorses. There, he demonstrated a car buffer, along with a special cleaning wax. He told his spectators, "Today and today only, if you buy a car buffer, we'll throw in a free bottle of cleaning wax." A lot of customers snapped up the offer, which underscored just how engaging and entrepreneurial Ricky could be when he applied himself.

Mom and Dad at one of B&G Hardware's annual Summer Sales Bonanzas.

Inside Mom's store, Bruce, one of the hardware supplier's salesmen, demonstrated a wood router—discounted for the bonanza—as "the perfect gift for your favorite woodworker." His job was to engrave each customer's name onto a small block of wood using the router. Karan had a table right next to Bruce's. The salesman would hand her the freshly engraved block of wood, and she would apply walnut-colored wood stain. My sister wasn't particularly artistic, but that wasn't the point. She was instructed to say, "Today and today only, select types of wood stain are marked down 20%." But for whatever reason, her sales pitch was less effective than Ricky's.

Meanwhile, Mom's two salesclerks roamed the aisles to help out customers and ring up sales on the cash register.

As for Mom, her job was to greet customers and hand them a free yardstick when they came through the door. Moments before her big bonanza debut, Mom cut open the boxes of yardsticks. As expected, one side had "B&G Hardware" printed on it. But when she flipped the yardstick over, the other side read, "Your Handy Helpful Hardware Man." She walked over to Bruce, the salesman, with a yardstick in her hand: "It says MAN!"

Bruce merely shrugged and told my mother to give out the yardsticks anyway—while "smiling real pretty." That made my mother even madder!

With no time to argue, she walked away in a huff. It was the height of the equal-rights era for women, when feminists like Gloria Steinem pushed for a constitutional amendment that would explicitly prohibit gender discrimination in areas like employment, education, insurance, federal contracts, and reproductive rights. It would also ban discriminatory lending practices in which women typically needed a male relative to co-sign on bank loans—including business loans. My mother was no rabble-rouser—she was essentially apolitical—but she firmly believed that women business owners should have the same rights as male-owned businesses.

Meanwhile, customers crowded around Ricky, who proceeded to buff a teeny-tiny patch of the car hood—so small, in fact, that it was hard to tell the difference between the "before" and "after." But Ricky had to take his time, because Mom advertised that the car-buffer demo would last all day long. He needed to save himself a swath of the grungy car hood for his afternoon crowds.

Inside the store, Bruce busily carved people's names into blocks of wood—including one for me with "Bethy" on it. There was only one snafu, and that's when a customer informed Bruce that her name was Charlotte. The block of wood wasn't long enough for all of the letters, so the woman's name had to go on two lines: "Char. . .lotte." Still, she was a good sport about it and told Bruce that it looked great, especially after Karan brushed walnut stain on it.

To her credit, my sister worked through the end of the day, even though her hands and blouse were covered with sticky residue from the wood stain. As for me, I was buzzing along after a day-long binge on Mountain Dew. What really mattered, though, was that the Spring Sales Bonanza was so successful that it became an annual event.

In the fall, Mom had an unplanned promotion that didn't involve the family whatsoever. It turned out to be one of her most successful advertising campaigns ever.

At the beginning of the school year, the careers teacher from the high school came to Mom's store to ask a favor. This instructor mainly worked with students who didn't see themselves as college material. Instead, he helped them find paid "internships" with local businesses in roles related to their interests. One of the instructor's students, a high school junior, said he was interested in both sales and marketing.

"Would you be willing to hire him for a semester and teach him about running a business?" the instructor asked.

Without hesitating, Mom said yes, explaining that a boss once took a chance on her when she was young.

The student's name was Kyle, and starting in late August, he worked three days a week at Mom's store instead of going to regular classes. The first time I was introduced to Kyle, he shook my hand, which caught me off guard because I was younger than he was. And even though we were meeting for the first time, I knew who Kyle was because his younger brother, Danny, was in the same grade as me. It was pretty easy to figure out that Kyle and Danny were brothers because they were Black. And there were hardly any Blacks—or other minorities, for that matter—at that time in McPherson.

My mom told Dad that she was "concerned" when Kyle first reported to work—not because he was Black. But because Kyle was very shy and soft-spoken, two qualities that she felt weren't ideal for a career in sales and marketing. At any rate, Mom had Kyle shadow her two part-time salesclerks, and he got to know the merchandise pretty quickly, considering he had never really been around hardware. The main challenge was getting Kyle to say,

"Can I help you?" loud enough for the customers to hear him.

When the hardware salesman made his weekly visit to Mom's store, Kyle shadowed my mother as she decided what seasonal merchandise to order for the fall—things like rakes, leaf bags, weather stripping, and a narrow scoop that cleans leaves out of the rain gutters.

Around this time, the manager of the local radio station came to the store offering Mom a chance to be part of a bold, new promotional campaign the station was having. For $500, my mom could air her own live radio show that would last one hour. During that time, the DJ would play any records she brought to the station. Between songs, Mom could talk about all of the good deals at B&G Hardware. Mom not only loved the idea, she thought it would be a great way for Kyle to learn about marketing.

Choosing the right records would be a delicate task, we decided, since some folks at church saw rock music as evil, a lesson I learned in Sunday School. My teacher cited some of the popular songs playing on the radio around then—titles like "Ring My Bell," "Lovin,' Touchin,' Squeezin," and "Hot Blooded." A sure sign that a song was sinful, the teacher continued, was when the music had a heavy backbeat. Then he played a cassette tape with clips of songs that he felt had a heavy backbeat. Next, he played songs that didn't have a heavy backbeat. Honestly, I couldn't discern the difference, which was unsettling to me. The teacher closed by asking us to join hands, close our eyes, and pray that Jesus would cleanse us of this scourge. Then he gave us a homework assignment. The following Sunday, we were told to bring to class at least one of our cassette tapes or record albums that he would burn on our behalf.

The teacher saw the record-burning exercise as a good way for us to demonstrate our faith. I saw the exercise as a good way to squander a perfectly good album. Still, I noticed that the other students were nodding their heads in agreement throughout the lesson. There was no way I could come to the next class empty-handed. At the time I probably had 20 albums in my collection, the first being a dorky Neil Diamond album that was a gift from my parents. (Meanwhile, Mom and Dad gave Karan an Olivia Newton John album, which made me insanely jealous.) If I showed up to the record-burning with the Neil Diamond album, everyone would know I was faking my faith. I realized that I had to choose an album that was two things:

1. Considered evil by my Sunday School teacher.
2. Would not be particularly missed by me if I subjected it to a fiery death.

Using those criteria, I narrowed my choice down to two albums. One was Gary Wright's *Dream Weaver* because it only had one good song on it. The other was *The Eagles Greatest Hits* because I wasn't crazy about any of their songs. I decided on the Eagles. It wouldn't be a big loss to me and—most important—I would earn me extra Jesus points because it was a *double album*.

I knew better than to ask my mother for her opinion. She couldn't stand Gary Wright, the Eagles, or many of the other big names in pop on KEYN, my favorite station. For her radio debut, Mom bought a dozen or so 45 rpm records—mostly oldies from the 1950s—from a local man who supplied juke boxes to bars, the bowling alley, truck stops, and other places.

On the day of the show, Kyle arrived at Mom's store with a stack of 3 x 5 index cards filled with bullet points related to hardware. Mom flipped through the cards, thinking it was "quaint" that someone would actually write down things to say about hardware. With all of the merchandise in her store, Mom was confident she would have no trouble speaking extemporaneously.

After they got to the radio station, Mom handed over the records to the station manager, who gave them to a DJ sitting in front of a turntable. The manager led Mom and Kyle into a different room that had a big glass window facing the DJ. Both Mom and Kyle had a microphone and a headset, and the manager gave them these instructions: The DJ would count down from five to one, and when he pointed at Betty, she'd be "live" on the air. If at any point my mom needed a little time to assemble her material, she could press a button on the desk that automatically switched over to a commercial. "But the ad is for some other business," the manager explained, "so don't press the button unless it's absolutely necessary. You're here to talk about B&G Hardware!"

Finally, it was go time. Mom and Kyle sat in their little room with the microphones and headsets. Using his fingers to count down, the DJ gestured, 5...4...3...2...1. Then he pointed directly at Mom. She froze, completely unable to form words with her mouth. She reached over and mashed the button, and the show went to a commercial for a Culligan water softener. Still, the ad break gave Mom enough time to collect her wits. As the commercial was ending, the DJ once again counted down 5...4...3...2...1 and pointed directly at Mom. Once again, her entire body became suddenly paralyzed. The DJ saw the panic on Mom's face, so he played one of her records, a Neil Diamond song. The manager brought a little paper cup of water into the room and asked, "Everything okay, Betty?" When she took the cup from him, the manager noticed that her hand felt like ice. But Mom said she would be fine once "Cracklin' Rose" finished playing. For the third time, the DJ counted down 5...4...3...2...1, but this time he pointed at Kyle. Without missing a beat, Kyle took on a big, brassy show-business voice, one that sounded exactly like a game show host's. Then Kyle started reading from his 3 x 5 cards: "It's autumn, and that means it's LEAF RAKING TIME! And B&G Hardware has a large assortment of rakes that will WHIP ANY YARD INTO SHAPE! Isn't that right, Betty?" My mother nodded her head, which didn't do much good for the listeners at home.

In between records, Kyle seamlessly filled the airwaves. He talked about the latest designs in Corning Ware casserole dishes. He said Frankoma Pottery's collectible plates made perfect hostess gifts. My mother was stunned by the transformation. She thought to herself, *How does Kyle—or any kid, really—know what a hostess gift is?*

From that point on, it was "The Kyle Show," starring *Mister Hardware*. In buttery tones that were completely new to Mom, Kyle told listeners how to take the squeak out of rusty hinges. He promoted a compound that filled chips in porcelain. He talked about power drills and circular saws, suggesting some simple DIY projects for his newest fans listening at home.

Just once, Kyle pressed the commercial button, and that's only because there was a minor slip-up with the music. One of Mom's 45's was "American Pie," the Don McClean song. The tune clocks in at almost 9 minutes. It was so long, in fact, that only half of it fit on the record's A-side. To hear the rest of it, you had to flip the record over to the B-side. The DJ didn't realize that, and he was completely flummoxed when "American Pie" abruptly ended halfway through. So, Kyle switched to a commercial to give the DJ time to figure out the problem. (Mom knew all along that the record needed to be flipped over but getting her to speak up would be like asking Doorknob to play a flute.) When the commercial ended, the DJ played the other half of "American Pie." Then Kyle leaned into the mic and said smooth as silk, "It's hard to say 'Bye-bye' to 'American Pie.'" He then closed the show, thanking all of his loyal listeners—who he hoped to see soon at B&G Hardware.

The next day at the store, there was a run on garden rakes, leaf bags, and other fall merchandise. Some people asked for Kyle by name. He had reverted to his old self, the soft-spoken Kyle that we first met, but he projected poise and professionalism that Mom hadn't noticed before.

From then on, she let Kyle work one-on-one with customers in his own quiet way, and his sales numbers were no different than when she had prodded him to be more bold and vocal.

At the end of the semester, when the teacher asked Mom to give Kyle a grade, she happily gave him an A.

I could see for myself that Mom's promotional efforts were paying off when I came to the store after school one day and saw a

Cadillac parked in her usual spot on the side of her building. Even though the car was "pre-owned," it was easily the classiest thing I had ever seen. The car was both wide and long, with a dusty mauve finish. Dad left his store and walked across the parking lot to take a look at it. He seemed just as pleased as Mom was.

"Let's take it to the Preserve Club!" I exclaimed. The Preserve was a public country club near Hutchinson, a larger town west of McPherson. My parents loved the idea. After the stores were locked up for the day, the four of us—Dad, Mom, Karan, and I—went home to put on our nicest clothes. We got in the car for our big night out. From our vantage point in the back seat, my sister and I were in awe of all the Cadillac's different knobs, buttons, and display lights. "It will take us a while to figure everything out," Mom said. But for the time being, we could all enjoy the ride—the Cadillac felt like we were floating on a cloud.

Without saying it aloud, Karan and I agreed that the best part about going to the Preserve Club was the arrival itself. When the car pulled up and stopped under the front awning, two really cute high school boys would run up to open the car doors for you. We stepped out of the car feeling like millionaires.

It took about 40 minutes for Dad to drive us from McPherson to the club. As he was pulling up under the awning, Mom told us, "Try to look calm, like young ladies." Dad stopped the car, and like clockwork, two really cute boys ran out to open our car doors. But when the boys pulled on the handles, nothing happened. All of the doors were locked! The four of us—even Dad—started pawing around the inside of the car to find the stems that are pulled up to unlock the doors. But the Cadillac didn't have stem locks. Soon, we were acting like caged animals, and the boys were peering at us through the windows like we were zoo monkeys. We were frantically—no, desperately—trying to figure out how to unlock the doors. After this went on for a while, the boys looked impatient. Using sweeping hand gestures, Dad communicated to the boys that he would park the car himself. Pulling out from under the awning,

I looked back and could see the boys laughing at us.

Unable to crawl onto the floorboard and quietly die, Karan and I mutely sat in the back seat, panting softly. Finally, we pulled into a parking spot that seemed like it was six miles away. Dad put the car in park and turned off the ignition. Like magic, all of the doors unlocked automatically. Then Dad shared this revelation: "I guess the car has to be in park for the doors to unlock. Under the awning, I was still in drive, with my foot on the brake."

"Maybe next time you should read the owner's manual first," I said helpfully. Mom and Dad turned and looked at me, and I could see little icy daggers shooting out of their eyes. I didn't care.

It felt like the whole world had witnessed my greatest humiliation. With that Cadillac, I thought our family had "arrived," both literally and figuratively. But when we couldn't even figure out how to unlock the doors to step into the country club, it felt like we were just posers.

It seemed that the more involved my parents got in the stores, the more they lost their handle on what was happening at home. Around the time he entered high school, Ricky started spending a lot more time with his friends than he was with me. His favorite thing to do was sneak out through his bedroom window at night. Many times, he met his friends at the city pool, which was just a few blocks away from our house. Since the pool was only open during the day, they had to climb over a chain-link fence to get in. Then they swam around in the dark, which would have terrified me. Making matters worse, all of them—girls included—stripped off their clothes before getting in the water so they wouldn't come home sopping wet. (And for other reasons, too, I'm sure.) His other schemes were increasingly suspicious. For example, he rode a mini-bike around the neighborhood, with vague explanations to my parents about where it actually came from.

And after he got his driver's license, Ricky installed a little toggle switch under the dashboard of Dad's pickup. When he flipped the switch, the taillights went off, even when the headlights were on. When Ricky borrowed the pickup, he used the switch to turn off the lights on the back of the truck, making it hard for other vehicles—a police car, for example—to follow him.

Karan was also headed for trouble. While prepping a load of laundry for the washing machine, my mother found a package of rolling papers used for making joints in my sister's jeans pocket. Taking a "scared straight" approach, my mother drove my sister to the police station and turned her in for drug possession. The officer explained that carrying rolling papers was not against the law. Nonetheless, my mother wouldn't let Karan leave the police station until she had divulged the name of the person who gave her the rolling papers. Eventually, my sister confessed: It was Ricky.

My parents suspected that both Ricky and Karan were dabbling in drugs, but they couldn't be sure. I had a pretty good clue, and once again, I got the hint in Sunday School. A member of our church—who was also a member of the sheriff's department—came to our Sunday School class to warn us about the evils of drugs. Even though it was Sunday and we were in church, the officer was dressed in full uniform, including a walkie-talkie and a Smokey the Bear-style hat. He set up a card table to display all sorts of drugs and paraphernalia that had been seized over the years by the sheriff's department. Our Sunday School teacher read a scripture verse from First Corinthians that read, in part, "Don't you know that your bodies are temples of the Holy Spirit?" She went on to explain how drugs defiled both your inner and your outer temple.

To help us spot drug-related danger signs, the officer pulled a little plastic baggie from his pocket that contained a white pill. It looked very much like an aspirin, but it wasn't. The officer took an ashtray off the table of drug paraphernalia and dropped the white pill into it. He struck a match and held the flame to the pill. It began to emit hazy white smoke, and before long, a pungent, skunky aroma filled the classroom. That pill, the officer told us, simulated the smell of marijuana when it was being smoked. I recognized that odor immediately from being around Ricky and Karan.

Class was almost over, so the officer extinguished the white pill. But there was still some time remaining for questions. He opened the floor, encouraging us to ask him anything. There was silence. He urged us on. "Come on, surely you have at least one question!" Again, more silence.

Finally, I took it upon myself to break the ice: "Officer Barry, if you were to take everything on that table there and sell it on the street, how much would it be worth?"

Silence.

Standing behind the table, the officer just glared at me, which I interpreted to mean that he didn't understand my question. So, I rephrased my query, hoping I would be clearer a second time. "Officer Barry, how much would the drugs and other stuff on your table be worth if you went out and tried to sell it?"

I hadn't even finished the question when the officer came out from around his table. As he slowly approached me, my voice started to falter. I was trying to spit out my words, even though the officer's face was red and his head quivered with rage. I was sitting on a metal folding chair, and the officer bent down so that the brim of his hat was pushing against my forehead. Finally, I finished my question, ". . .be worth if you went out and tried to sell it?" The officer's face was so close to mine, I watched only his mouth as he hissed, "NOTHING, if you're a GOD. FEARING. CHRISTIAN!"

With that, my most pious classmate thrust her arm high into the air—her hand cupped and swiveling like a human satellite dish searching for a signal. "YES, Jesus! THANK YOU, Jesus!" she exclaimed.

Once again, my big mouth had gotten me into trouble. I'm sure the sheriff knew that I was a Copeland. There was even a chance that some of the drug paraphernalia displayed on the card table had been confiscated from Ricky.

"Was that why the sheriff shouted at me like that?" I later asked a friend in the class. I would never know the answer.

Ricky's final infraction put my parents over the brink. The cash register in the auto parts department had been coming up short for quite some time, so Dad secretly installed a security camera in his store to figure out why. When he reviewed the footage, he learned Ricky was the one stealing the money.

After my folks discovered the theft, Dad said he was "putting his foot down." Ricky swore he'd never do another dishonest thing for the rest of his life.

But first, Ricky told me he had one more money-making plan. And he needed my help. My brother wanted to buy two or three condom machines and install them in the *women's* restrooms at a few bars around town. Here's the catch: Ricky wouldn't actually stock the machines with condoms, because "no respectable woman in Kansas would walk out to the bartender and complain, 'Hey, I put 50 cents in the condom machine, but I didn't get a condom!'" The scheme had low overhead, Ricky explained, because all he had to do was occasionally collect the quarters from his machines. Basically, he was taking advantage of polite society.

The plan had a problem, though. He needed "seed money" to buy the condom machines. Since Dad was wise to his schemes, Ricky decided that I was the best person to ask Dad to fund our project because I was younger and "looked innocent."

But before I could go to my dad, I had one quick question: "What the heck is a condom?" Before Ricky could explain the purpose of a condom, he first had to explain "the facts of life" to me. He launched into a windy description about how man parts and lady parts connect—which at the time sounded like the most ridiculous thing I had ever heard. I repeated his account to Mom, and I was shocked when she said Ricky was right! That gave my mother the opportunity to *demonstrate* the birds and the bees for me. Her props: two metal pipe fittings, which have a "male" and a "female" end.

At any rate, I got cold feet about Ricky's plan once I knew what a condom was. In fact, I was starting to feel uncomfortable with a lot of his other schemes. So were my parents. Off and on for the next few weeks, there was lots of shouting among the three of them, but I was never told the details. But finally, Mom, Dad and Ricky came to an agreement.

About a 45-minute drive north of McPherson, where I-135 meets up with I-70, is a town called Salina. Mom and Dad decided that Salina held the key to getting Ricky back on track. With a bleak future ahead in McPherson, Ricky agreed. So, one Sunday in late May, we all got in the car and drove to Salina to drop off Ricky. When he came back to the car to say goodbye, Ricky's head had been shaved so his hair was roughly the length of peach fuzz. The next day, he started summer school and what would be his junior year at an all-boys military school.

Right then, it felt like my best friend had died.

7.
THE MAGIC OF HELLO DOLLIES

While Ricky was being shipped off to military school, Ronnie was graduating from high school. Soon, he would be leaving home too.

My father had a saying about my oldest brother: "Ron was 40 the day he was born."

Serious, studious, and even-tempered, Ronnie was different from the rest of us kids, almost like he came from a different family.

And everyone knew that he was more religious than the rest of us. Once, one of Ricky's friends, a boy named Doug, came to our house with a Ouija board, which supposedly communicated with the dead. We all put our fingers on the planchette, the pointer that spells out messages from the "spirits," and asked a bunch of silly questions. Then, Doug asked the spirits this one: "How is Bethy going to die?"

Very slowly, the planchette moved across the board and spelled "D....R....O....W....N."

Spooked, I didn't want to play anymore after that. Just about then, Ronnie walked into the room and saw what we were doing. Without hesitating, he pushed the planchette aside, picked up the Ouija board, and snapped it over his knee.

"Hey, that's mine!" Doug protested.

"I really don't care," Ronnie snapped back.

Rarely did my brother lash out that way, but I believe he was trying to save us from participating in something he considered so sinful. He wasn't proselytizing, he was acting on his beliefs.

Ronnie had one more summer in McPherson before heading

off to college at the University of Kansas in Lawrence.

That summer, my dad didn't have a bookkeeper at his store for whatever reason, so my brother agreed to handle the office work. The financial side of Dad's business was a mystery to me, so I asked Ronnie if I could be his helper. He agreed.

I'm sure I wasn't the easiest kid to deal with, especially after hanging out with Ricky so much. But Ronnie was patient, and he talked to me almost like I was grown up.

I started out on basic tasks—things like filing sales tickets and stuffing envelopes with the monthly statements. He must have known that I was getting restless, so he tried to make my work more challenging. For example, he filled out a bank deposit slip each morning, listing the cash and checks taken in the previous day. These amounts were totaled up on an adding machine. Ronnie's fingers moved so rapidly on the keys, it sounded like he was firing a tiny machine gun. I was in awe that he didn't have to look at the numbers.

Then my brother would give me the deposit slip, and I had to use the adding machine to come up with the same total he had. I rolled my chair over to the adding machine and used the hunt-and-peck method to enter in the numbers. When my total didn't match his, Ronnie made me run the numbers again—however many times as it took for me to get it right.

I was so impressed with Ronnie's dexterity on the adding machine, I wanted to learn to use it without looking at the numbers, just like he did. I found some blank stickers and stuck them over all of the number buttons. I wouldn't be able to cheat by peeking. I did the same with the two adding machines behind the front checkout counter—and even on the cash register's number keypad. That way, *everybody* could learn how to punch in numbers without looking. As one might expect, there were lots of complaints from the staff.

But of course, I couldn't stop there. I realized that the push buttons on the telephone had three rows of three buttons, just like an adding machine. But the phone's buttons were the inverse of those on the adding machine. That is, the top row of the phone's keypad is 1-2-3. The top row of an adding machine is 7-8-9. So, I stuck the little stickers to cover up the numbers on all of the telephones. That way, *everybody* could learn how to make a call without looking at the numbers.

My latest move started a minor employee revolt. My efforts to work faster were making everyone else work slower. My dad lowered the boom, "Bethy, I want you to remove every single sticker. You're being a nuisance and getting on everyone's nerves."

That last phrase—getting on everyone's nerves—struck me. It hadn't occurred to me how my actions were affecting everyone else. Back in the office, I asked Ronnie, "Do you think I'm annoying?"

His answer? "Sometimes."

He was being honest, at least. When I acted impulsively or I got sassy with someone, Ronnie explained, I could be hurtful. Not only was that wrong, he continued, it changed how other people thought of me.

"Wouldn't it be nice if people described you as thoughtful and kind?" he said.

Ouch.

All the things we talked about stuck in my brain. And as the summer progressed, he gave increasingly difficult challenges. What charge accounts had overdue balances? What would those balances be with a 1.5 percent late fee? Did our total receipts for the month exceed the amount spent on payroll, freight orders, utilities, and other expenses? How much did customers pay in sales tax?

I got frustrated when I couldn't come up with the answers. How was I supposed to know? I wasn't going to major in business like he was. One day, I got so fed up, I told him, "I quit!"

But instead of begging me to stay, Ronnie replied, "You don't quit. You're fired!" That made me even madder, and I stomped off in a huff. The next day, I came back into the office and Ronnie said, "What are you doing here? I fired you, remember?" So, I stomped off again.

Eventually, Ronnie tracked me down at Mom's store and said, "You can come back. But first, you have to ask me *nicely* for your job back." He must have known that I was ready to eat crow.

"May I have my job back?" I asked.

"Yes."

That's all he said— "yes." There was no anger, no smugness. I went back to the office, and the matter never came up again. (That is, until years later. Every now and then he reminds me of the day he fired me.)

The night before Ronnie left for college, Mom made a big supper and served his favorite dessert, German chocolate cake. It was delicious—once I picked out the coconut.

The next morning, my brother packed up his Buick Opel and said his goodbyes. Then he pulled me aside, saying he had a special gift, just for me.

"What is it?" I asked, thinking it would be something related to my bookkeeping duties that summer.

"You can have my bedroom," he said.

I almost cried. Sharing a room with Karan had become unbearable, and I'm sure the feeling was mutual. She was a night owl, and I was an early bird. She was a slob, and I was a neat freak. She liked Led Zeppelin, and I liked James Taylor.

With Ronnie's stuff cleared out, I could have my own space. I hung up my posters of Tweetie Bird and Pigs in Space. My record player sat atop a milk crate filled with albums, alphabetized, of course. And Tetsy, my red stuffed teddy bear that had been with me since infancy, leaned against my pillow. But the walls were a mossy green color and pretty scuffed up.

Mom thought this would be a good opportunity for me to learn a new skill at the store: tinting paint.

I wasn't what you would call a fast learner. Mom and Dad

carried different brands of paint, but the method used to tint it was basically the same. Customers flipped through a book of paint chips to pick their desired shade. Underneath the paint chip was the formula for tinting a can of neutral paint base. The base was either for interior or exterior use, and it came in a number of finishes, such as flat and gloss. The pigment was mixed into the base, and the result was checked for accuracy before it was handed over to the customer.

For my new bedroom, I picked a shade of yellow called "Lemon Drop." The color chip called for one little plastic container of #318, and one larger plastic container of #814. I used a church key—a type of bottle opener—to pry the lids off two cans of interior base paint in a flat finish. Then, I dumped in the containers of powdered pigment. The lids went back on the cans and were banged shut with a rubber mallet. One at a time, each can was tipped on its side and clamped onto the paint shaker, with the timer set for three minutes.

I took the cans of paint home on a Saturday so Dad and I could tackle the project the next day. Of course, my first step was to place my most valuable possessions—my collection of James Taylor albums—inside a closet to protect them from drips. Then Dad and I moved everything else away from the walls and covered the furniture with plastic drop cloths. Using a paintbrush, I cut in around the trim, while Dad painted the rest of the walls using a roller.

After he finished the first can of paint, he opened the second can and started rolling it on the wall. But the color in this can didn't look at all like Lemon Drop. This hue was a sickly yellow, somewhat akin to the color of urine. Dad poked around inside the can with a wooden paint-stirrer, and he could see clumps of #318 and #814 that hadn't been evenly disseminated. Obviously, I had neglected one critical step: Once the paint came off the shaker, I failed to remove the lid and inspect the color inside to make sure it matched the color on the paint chip.

At this point, it would have been impossible to re-tint the second can so that it matched the color in the first can. My father was noticeably annoyed.

"This has been a complete waste of time!" he barked, spittle spraying from his mouth.

Mom drove to her store—even though Sundays were her only day off—and mixed up two more cans of Lemon Drop. This time, they matched. Then we had to paint over our earlier work.

Not long after messing up my bedroom paint, I made an even bigger mistake. A customer came into Dad's store for interior latex, picking out a tan-colored paint chip. I dumped the pigment into the base paint and banged the lid shut with the mallet. I clamped the can on the shaker, set the timer for 3 minutes and turned on the machine. The moment the paint shaker started doing its thing, the lid unexpectedly flew off the can! It only took me a few seconds to reach over and turn the shaker off, but by then, the customer and I looked like we had taken a swim in a vat of gravy. Hearing the commotion, Dad came into the paint room and saw the paint-splattered aftermath. This time, however, he didn't yell at me. Instead, he stood in stunned silence.

In addition to mixing paint, my parents wanted me to learn other new skills, very few of which I put to use today. At Mom's store, I used a machine that manually duplicated keys. To cut copper tubing, I used a tool that was lightly clamped on the pipe and turned by hand while a sharp wheel cut through the soft metal. I cut nylon rope on a little gizmo with a red-hot blade that basically burned the piece of rope off the spool. That way, the end of the rope was melted so it wouldn't unravel. Sisal rope, meanwhile, was cut with a pocket knife. Plastic sheeting on giant rolls was unfurled and cut with a box knife. Mesh screen was cut with long shears, as was asbestos paper that people once used to retard fire. Tin snips cut chicken wire, and bolt cutters cut chain.

My father also taught me some basic home repairs. He showed me how to replace window screens using a tool called a spline roller. Similarly, I learned how glazing points worked when replacing a pane of glass in a window. I replaced faucet washers and put a new fitting on the end of a garden hose using a worm-gear clamp. (A surprising number of people smash the ends of their hoses when they drive over them with the car.)

He showed me how to add a switch to a cord by splitting the "hot" and "neutral" wires. I practiced by adding a switch to a light fixture in my bedroom. It worked great—for a while. When the fixture stopped working, I took the switch apart, thinking that one of the wires had come loose. Even after tightening the connection and reassembling the switch, the light still didn't work when I plugged it in. That's when I took the switch apart again and called my dad into the room. He took one look at my handiwork and left for a bit. When he came back, he had a new light bulb in his hand. Voila! I had overlooked the obvious problem, a burned-out bulb.

Ready access to the merchandise was perhaps the greatest advantage of being the daughter of two hardware store owners. One of my little projects led to a domestic squabble—with me at the center of the dispute. I had purchased a beat-up oak table and four matching chairs at a garage sale, and they were badly in need of refinishing. I could get the materials—wood filler, sandpaper, stripper, stain, etc.—at Mom's store for the low price of free. That beat out my dad, who carried different brands of basically the same supplies, but only with the 20% family discount. On Sundays, I hauled the table out of the barn in the backyard and set it on the back patio. While my parents watched me work from the sofa inside, they quibbled over almost every detail of the project—from the sandpaper grit, to the types of brushes, to the polyurethane finish. The table turned out great, but I didn't bring any more DIY projects home.

Over time, I must have given off a small whiff of hardware expertise myself, because my friends' parents and even some teachers would ask me questions related to their repairs. My seventh-grade math teacher once called me up to his desk, and in low tones asked which fasteners best resisted rust and corrosion. The next day I brought him a selection of brass wood screws. He picked the four that he needed, and I filled out a sales ticket—and calculated the tax!—so he could pay me. Another time, I was about to head to a friend's house for a sleepover. Before I left, my friend's mom called me at the store, asking me to bring four AA batteries with me. I took the batteries with me to the sleepover, along with the correct change for her $20 bill.

I was also increasingly able to make chit-chat with the regular customers. Knowing someone's name was not only considerate, it made customers feel good when they came into the stores. Sometimes I would even horse around on the intercom system at Dad's store, loudly calling out the names of customers as they walked in the door. Making my voice sound like a baseball announcer's, I would say, "Jon BERRRR-gerrrr!" "BRI-an HOST!" "Jo-DEEEEE Schlehuber!"

I was particularly charming when a cute boy came into the store. True, I was new to the whole boyfriend game, and I doubted I was much of a catch compared to the cheerleader-types at school. Happily, I was well past "the ugly years," as my dad called them. But even so, I was pretty plain. I didn't wear makeup, I wore practical clothes, and my figure had a certain corn-fed beef look to it. Not helping my cause were metal braces on my teeth, along with rubber bands attached to the wires to realign my jaw.

But do you know who thought I was beautiful? Arthur, from the peanut gallery, thought I was beautiful. And smart. And funny. And kind.

As I got older, Arthur and the rest of the coffee drinkers didn't torment me the way they used to. They swept up the peanut shells themselves and filled up the peanut pan when it got low. I didn't have to make coffee anymore, and one of them—I never knew who—set out doughnuts when my birthday came around. And when it snowed, I'd go out to my car at the end of the day and find that the ice had been scraped off my windshield.

Using my mouthiest tone, I would ask the old men, "Okay, which one of you got a brain transplant?"

Nobody would ever confess.

Arthur appointed himself my wingman and was determined to find me the boy of my dreams. And while sitting by the coffee pot, quietly cracking open peanuts, he applied a number of tests to determine whether a boy was worthy of my affections.

Boys were quickly eliminated if they snickered about naughty hardware names. If, for example, a customer walked up to me and said, "I'd like an eight-inch screw," he was scratched off the potential-boyfriend list. Ditto with, "Do you have four-inch nipples?"

It's shocking how many double entendres exist in the world of hardware. To name a few, there are bastard files and butt hinges, stud finders, jam nuts, and shank washers. And don't forget ballcocks, tongue-and-groove router bits, naval jelly, pipe dope, and penetrating oil.

A sloppy appearance was another no-go. Arthur rejected one of my classmates who came into the store covered in grease and grime. Clearly the boy had been helping his dad on the farm. But the dirt was unacceptable to Arthur.

"His parents must hide his Christmas presents in the bathtub," Arthur observed. "He'll never find them in there."

Another boy was judged a possible yes, even though he occasionally said "damn." But the moment Arthur discovered that the boy used chewing tobacco, he was deemed unworthy. On a few occasions, a boy would come through the door who was clean, polite, and had a friendly smile. When that happened, Arthur would steer him over to me so I could wait on him. After the boy left, Arthur would ask me in front of my dad and everybody for a thumbs-up or a thumbs-down assessment, which embarrassed me terribly.

I don't think my dad was ready for me to date, and I know that my mother didn't want me going out. They each had their own reasons. Dad's only requirements were that the boy had to be gainfully employed and have clean fingernails. But he was dismissive of a lot of the boys from my school.

"They're all hat and no horse," he told me.

There was some truth to that. At school, we had a term for boys who dressed like cowboys but had never stepped foot onto a farm: "goat ropers." They wore tooled-leather belts with big metal buckles and cowboy boots with pointy toes. Typically, there was a can of Skoal nestled deep in their back pockets. It was a popular look back then, but it seemed to me like goat ropers were pretending to be someone they weren't.

My mother didn't want me dating boys because she was afraid I'd be seduced and get pregnant. To her, being a virgin was about the holiest thing a girl could be.

Meanwhile, she suspected that Karan's virginity was a moot point when my sister came home one Saturday night with her shirt inside out. Lucky for her, Dad wasn't around to notice that Karan's buttons were facing inward.

If Dad knew Karan was having sex, he would blow his stack. But Mom had to be realistic. She didn't want Karan to bear the burden of a teen pregnancy. Broaching the subject with my father would require the poise and tact of a senior diplomat.

At bedtime one night, she turned to him and said, "I think Karan's moods could be improved if she went on birth-control pills."

"What does the pill have to do with Karan's moods?" he asked incredulously.

"It stabilizes her hormone levels so she doesn't have such wild mood swings," Mom replied.

As a matter of fact, the pill could help with Karan's moods. Her PMS symptoms were so severe every month that Ricky diagnosed her with Mad Cow Disease.

There were probably other girls in high school who were using the pill as a birth-control method, but they would never admit it.

My high school was the kind of place where *all* of the boys had had sex, but *none* of the girls had. That led to a lot of speculation as to who was lying. In my senior year, one of my classmates got pregnant. And when I told my mom later that day, she asked, "How did that happen?" To which I replied, "Mother, I think it's time you and I had a little talk." I was ready to break out the pipe fittings for the visual demo.

While my parents knew I had plenty of growing up to do, they were ready to give me more responsibility. For example, Mom started scheduling her appointments and errands after I got out of school so I could keep her store humming along while she was out.

One regular visit was to the hair salon, where June, her longtime stylist, would comb and tease Mom's hair into a fluffy bouffant. That was followed by a fog of hairspray to stiffen the hairdo into something akin to a helmet. Throughout the drawn-out process, both June and Mom smoked and drank coffee, swapping stories about happenings around town. Neither woman was a petty gossip. They just updated each other on the latest family news going around.

A true test of my abilities came one February when my parents took a rare weeklong vacation to an auto parts convention in Hawaii. My father surprised my mom at Christmas with airline tickets to Honolulu.

"Is it too late to get a refund?" was Mom's first question. But eventually she warmed to the idea.

Jenny and Heyfae could easily keep Dad's store going. They basically worked in sync like they were the same person. But Mom only had two part-time clerks who worked on alternating days. So, while Mom was in Hawaii, I was given the responsibility of opening up B&G Hardware at 8 a.m. Once her clerk got to work, I left for school. When classes ended, I went back to the store and worked until closing time at 6 p.m.

I felt grown up and responsible. Like a business mogul. Like someone who would walk into a doughnut shop and order a cappuccino. Or, more simply, like someone who had graduated from her training bra.

At some point during the week—while my parents were in balmy Hawaii—a major snowstorm swept across Kansas, dumping over 10 inches of snow. For the next two days, both stores were busy, busy, busy as people dug out from the storm. Shovels and snowplows worked non-stop. Homeowners salted their stoops and sidewalks. And plumbers jumped in to make repairs after water pipes froze.

One afternoon, one of my mother's clerks said there was a telephone call for the manager. I went to the office and a reporter from the *Hutchinson News* was on the line. Her assignment was to contact area merchants to see how they were handling the fallout from the storm. The reporter asked me a few questions, and I answered the best I could. Her last one was, "How old are you?" By the tone of her voice, I sensed that she was sneering at me.

In the following day's newspaper, I saw this headline: "Patrons Are Intent on Shoveling Out." Deep in the story was this paragraph:

Beth Copeland, 14-year-old manager of B&G Hardware at McPherson said the companion shop, Copeland Supply, sold "about 30 snow shovels Thursday, three or four snow blowers and lots of tire chains."

Readers must have wondered, *How could it be that a 14-year-old is managing a hardware store? Is she even old enough to drive?* More curiously, *Why is she talking about snow-shovel sales at a different hardware store than the one she manages?* And just to pick nits, *Shouldn't there be a comma after the word McPherson?*

Reading that paragraph, however, I had a completely different reaction: I felt like a foolish little kid. Why did she have to include my age in the article? Nobody else's age was given in the piece. By giving the interview, I was hoping the store would get some publicity, but now nobody would take it seriously.

There was a painful truth to my embarrassment. Yes, I was opening and closing my mother's hardware store. But the very capable salesclerks were dealing with most of the customers, handling freight deliveries, writing up orders for the wholesaler, and making bank deposits in the mornings. That's because good business owners work hard to hire good employees who can take care of business when they're away.

When my parents returned home from Hawaii, they told me how they went to a luau, tasted poi, and saw a whale breach while on a boating excursion. My mother marveled that the airplane had 10 seats across. But it was the last vacation Mom ever took. She had a great time in Hawaii, but nobody—myself included—could manage her store the way she wanted.

About this time, I began to notice a boy from church coming into Dad's place to pick up parts for his father's machine shop. He was three years older than me, so we didn't share any classes in high school. We were both active in the church youth group, which met on Sunday evenings, and in the youth choir, which practiced on Wednesday nights. His name was Jon, and he was funny and smart, but what I liked most was that he was incredibly kind to everyone.

He was also religious but not self-righteous. There were no windy prayers before choir practice, and he wasn't embarrassed to help the women with the dishes after potluck suppers. Little kids and old people alike were drawn to him, which is always a good sign.

Jon occasionally came into Dad's store to pick up some items, and every now and then he would grab a pop from the machine and hang out with the old coffee drinkers. He knew everybody by name and was completely at ease talking and laughing with people who were at least 40 years older than he was. As for Arthur, it didn't take long for him to realize that I had a crush on Jon.

It was pretty obvious to everyone, actually, because I got noticeably flustered whenever Jon came in. One time, he needed some bolts in the back, and I stepped forward to help him find the right fasteners, which of course was just an excuse. As I rounded the checkout counter, I slammed into a tall rack of circular-saw blades, and the whole lot came crashing down. Luckily, each blade was shrink wrapped on cardboard. Had they been loose, I might have lost a few toes. Another time, Jon came in when I was writing up a sales ticket for another customer. I needed to attach the man's purchase order to his sales ticket, and the stapler was in a drawer that could be a little sticky. I opened the drawer and pulled out a stapler, then I leaned hard on the drawer to make it shut—mashing my fingertips in the process. I kept my composure, hoping Jon hadn't seen my mishap. Of course, Arthur saw everything. Later that day, he asked me, "How are those fingers doing?" When I looked down, some of my nails were starting to blacken.

One day Jon came into the store and needed help finding 3/4-inch ready rod, which is a 3-foot piece of metal with top-to-bottom threads. Dad kept the ready rod in the bolt room, and Jon must have known it was there since he had walked past it at least a dozen times. Regardless, I led him to where the ready rod was located and turned to go back up front to the checkout counter. Jon lightly touched my arm and said, "Wait just a minute." My face flushed. "I'm wondering if you'd like to go to the Brookville Hotel with me on Saturday?"

Jon asking me to go to a hotel sounded presumptuous, but it wasn't. The Brookville Hotel was a beloved restaurant in Central Kansas that was famous for its fried-chicken dinners served family style. (My mother was so fond of the creamed corn there that she asked them for the recipe.) The restaurant was almost an hour's drive north of McPherson, so I was flattered that Jon would want to take the trouble for a first date.

Brookville was located along the Kansas Pacific Railroad, and the town was founded by some railroad workers in 1870. In 1980, when I went there with Jon, only about 250 souls lived there, and Main Street was not even paved.

We decided on a time for Jon to pick me up at my house. Happily, he already knew where I lived, so I didn't have to give him my address on Hartup Street, which is pronounced "hard up street." To me, "hard-up" reeked of distress and desperation. The only street in town with a worse name than Hartup was Skancke Street, which, yes, is pronounced "skanky."

I was quiet in the car, nervous that I would somehow embarrass myself. So, Jon asked me one question after another to draw me out of my shell.

"Are you going to the chili supper at church next week?"

"Did you hear about the fire west of town?"

"Who's trying out for basketball this year?"

If I had been a contestant on *The Dating Game*, the bachelor would have thought I was an empty chair concealed behind the screen.

But then Jon casually mentioned a new technology that could someday help farmers work their fields more efficiently. It involved installing a global-positioning device on their tractors. Satellite signals would guide farmers as they worked their land—tilling the soil, planting seed, harvesting crops—helping them get higher yields with their crops. Jon's dad was experimenting with some GPS devices in his shop.

It was fascinating, and I had a million questions. How did the GPS devices connect to the satellites? Were the tractors automated when they moved, or did the farmer still have to turn the steering wheel? Was the technology just for new tractors, or could older models be retrofitted with GPS? Jon didn't know all of the answers—the development of this technology for use in agriculture was still in its infancy. But we chattered about the possibilities all through supper and for most of the hour-long drive back to my house. In just one evening, I went from merely "smitten" to unequivocally "head over heels."

When we got back to my house, Jon walked me up to my porch to say goodnight. There, he paused to ask me, "Do you mind if I kiss you?" Once again, I succumbed to the flibbertigibbets, but somewhere in my torrent of words, I said "yes." What he said next came as a surprise.

"Well, first, I have to tell you something," Jon said.

"Really? What is it?" I replied, somewhat bewildered.

"I want you to know that I have diabetes," he said, "and the medicine that I take gives me *really chapped lips*."

Then, Jon pulled me up to him and kissed me for a long time. I know I should have been swooning at that moment, but Jon's lips felt very rough, almost like terry cloth. After the kiss, when he drew back, I could feel the little flakes of his lips that had been left behind on mine. It was difficult, but I resisted the urge to wipe my mouth off with the back of my hand. I didn't really want another kiss, so I launched into my "thanks" and "good-nights" to end the date. I clearly wasn't the most mature girl in the world, because the moment I felt his furry, flaky lips, the romantic spell was broken. Jon and I still talked on the phone occasionally, but soon after that kiss, we decided we wanted to be "just friends."

The following Monday at Dad's store, I could see that Arthur was waiting for me to give him a full report. I knew if I told him about the flaky lips, Arthur would see me as shallow and heartless. I mean, Jon couldn't help it that he had diabetes, after all. So, I never revealed to Arthur what had happened. All I said was, "I had a really nice time, but I don't think anything will come of it."

"Beth Copeland, please report to the principal's office," blared the intercom during my second-period English class.

"Oooooooooooo," my classmates scolded in unison, knowing that I must be in trouble.

I couldn't imagine what I had done wrong. I was still

rewinding my mental videotape for some clues when the teacher said, "Beth, you better get going."

When I walked into the principal's office, I saw my mother standing by a supply closet, waiting for me. That further confused me. Why would she be here so early in the day? Mom pulled me into the closet and shut the door. "Bethy, there's been an accident, and your father is hurt." By the look on her face, I knew it was bad.

My father had gone to the steel shop at the back of his building to retrieve something stored on top of a rack of metal flatbar, she explained. He leaned a tall, wooden ladder against the rack and started climbing. As he neared the top, the rung he was standing on snapped in two, and my father lost his balance. As the ladder began to fall, my father desperately tried to grab onto the flatbar rack. But he couldn't, so he plunged in a free fall toward the concrete floor roughly 20 feet below. His body landed on a small pile of metal that had been set out for delivery.

Later, I heard more details from the guys in the steel shop. George the Welder ran to my father's side and found him conscious, but in excruciating pain. George told Cookie to call an ambulance, then stay with Dad until it arrived. George hurried across the parking lot and found my mother at her store.

"There's been an accident, and Cope is hurt," he said.

Mom dropped what she was doing, and they both rushed over to the steel shop. There, she found my dad begging Cookie to remove the metal from underneath him. But my mother wouldn't allow it, fearful that moving my father would only worsen his injuries. By that time, sirens were blaring in the distance as the ambulance made its way to the store. Cookie stood in the street to block traffic, and he directed the ambulance to the alley behind the building—it was closest to the steel shop.

The medics jumped from the ambulance and ran into the steel shop, where they immediately saw the broken ladder and my father lying on the ground. Moving my father was going to be tricky, the EMTs told my mother, because there were most likely broken bones and possibly internal injuries. The lead EMT was feeling around my father's arms and legs to identify any immediate issues. While doing this, he instructed the other medic to run to the ambulance and get a neck brace, a backboard, and a gurney. At that moment, they both glanced up to see that the ambulance was rolling down the alley. They had forgotten to put the vehicle in park!

The lead EMT dropped the limb he had been examining—causing my father to cry out in pain—and he and his partner chased the ambulance down the alley. Fortunately, they were able to stop it before anybody else got hurt. It was a long, laborious process to apply the neck brace and gently slide my father onto a backboard to secure his spine. As they worked, my father complained of difficulties breathing.

My mother followed the ambulance to the hospital and met with the emergency room doctor after he had examined my father. Dad's injuries were severe, the doctor said, but they didn't appear to be life-threatening. Dad was given pain medication and taken to the hospital's radiology department so his entire body could be X-rayed. Knowing that it would take time to get the results, my mother got back into her car and drove to my school. That's when the principal's office pulled me from English class.

Mom wanted to tell me about the accident as soon as possible, because in a small town, news travels fast. And each time the story is relayed to someone new, the details inadvertently change along the way. My mother wanted to be the first to tell me before somebody mistakenly told me that Dad was found dead in a pool of his own blood.

After our tete-a-tete in the supply closet, I asked Mom if I could go with her back to the hospital, even if it meant just sitting in the waiting room. She agreed, saying that while I waited, she would go to the emergency room in case she was needed. After what seemed like hours, she returned to share the results with me. The news was promising, Mom said. Some of Dad's ribs were broken, making it painful for him to breathe. Beyond that, he suffered significant bruising and some scrapes and cuts. The news was a big relief. Still, there was a chance he had undetected internal injuries, so the ER doctor admitted him to the hospital for a few days.

Mom and I went up to Dad's room and found the curtains drawn, the lights dimmed. With every breath, my father moaned. Dad was heavily medicated, the nurse said, so he wasn't able to talk much. The only thing I could do was stand by the bed and hold my father's hand.

The next person to arrive was our pastor. When something bad happens in a small town like McPherson, somebody, somewhere knows to call your pastor. He didn't stay long—just enough time to give Dad some encouragement and pray for his strength and healing. By nighttime, there wasn't much we could do by sticking around while Dad slept. Mom and I got back in the car and headed to her store only to find that somebody—probably Jenny or Heyfae—had already turned out the lights and locked the doors.

When we got back to the house, we found grocery sacks, casserole dishes, and even a puzzle book on the front porch. Among them were several hand-written notes from members of our church family, each expressing their hopes for Dad's speedy recovery. People had been stopping by throughout the afternoon to leave us meals, snacks, iced tea, and, of course, multiple pans of Hello Dollies, our favorite cookie bars.

Hello Dollies were a kind of currency in our community. Once, when Karan accidentally broke something in a local store, my mother called the owner to ask what she owed him. The response: a pan of Hello Dollies. Another time, a woman's car hit and killed one of our cats as it crossed the street. The next day she came to our house with a pan of Hello Dollies.

When my dad got hurt, a huge, invisible safety net swooped underneath our feet to catch us. With no prompting from the pastor, the town just stepped up and started baking, and people just continued dropping things off at the house in the following days.

Jenny and Heyfae were firmly at the helm at Dad's store, and I went there after school to help out. However, I dreaded going back on the first day after Dad's accident—because I knew what awaited me. It happened anytime anybody had any sort of accident.

I walked in the door, and the moment I got near the coffee pot, Arthur and the other coffee drinkers wanted a full report on Dad's condition and recovery. With those niceties out of the way, they could now launch into *The Industrial Accident Horror Show*. Their material was drawn from years of experience working on farms, in oil fields, and with heavy machinery.

The *Horror Show* worked like this: Basically, one guy started by saying, "You think Cope's injury was bad? I know a guy who was taking an air conditioner out of a second-story window. He fell off the ladder onto the ground, then the air conditioner fell on top of him!"

"Well, you think that's bad," another continued, "I know a man who fell off his tractor when he was disking his field. The tractor kept moving forward, and one of the disks cut off his hand!"

It's a storytelling competition, with each account becoming exponentially more gruesome than the one before it. I could feel my loins drawing up within me. My breaking point usually came with the story of the guy who got his shirtsleeve caught in a lathe.

"Let's say we all go back to talking about the weather," I said encouragingly. It was too soon to hear these harrowing stories after what Dad had gone through.

Soon, my father's pain was under control. Nonetheless, he was in no hurry to leave the hospital. He was enjoying the attention. Everyone from church, the stores, and elsewhere in town was coming by to visit him.

"Bethy, they're bringing me sappy cards and candy bars and telling me how much they love me," Dad marveled.

His accident pre-dated insurance-company rules that have since made hospital stays much shorter. A lot of patients are eager to get back home. But not my father. He loved the TLC. Lucky for him, the hospital kept him for seven days.

My father had been back at work for a couple of weeks since his accident, and he still had pain and some physical limitations, such as difficulty lifting and carrying boxes. With him on the sidelines I needed to be on hand for Thanksgiving week, when he conducted his annual inventory. It also happened to be the week Arthur jokingly called "hunting season."

Inventory was a colossal task, so every year my father hired a dozen or so students who attended Central College, one of the liberal arts colleges in town. Most of the students who helped with inventory had families that lived out of state, so they were stuck in Mac through the holiday break. Arthur saw this as an opportunity to field romantic prospects on my behalf. Just being college students automatically made them eligible candidates for me, Arthur said. And since they were older, he felt they had more maturity than some of the high school kids who came in. I reminded him that college students most likely wanted to date other college students, but Arthur was undaunted.

That year, one particular college student shot to the top of Arthur's list. I am certain it's because the guy had a British accent. I can't remember his name, just his posh accent. "Oliver" sounds about right.

My father assigned Oliver to count all of the items related to electrical work—fuses, switches, wire strippers, and the like. Listening in, Arthur stepped forward to suggest that I write down Oliver's totals on a clipboard after he had counted the items.

"It will make the process more efficient," Arthur told Oliver.

Well, I have to hand it to Arthur. He picked a good one. Taking inventory doesn't exactly lend itself to long conversations, but from what I could tell, Oliver was what Arthur called "the total package." Cute, smart, and witty. And let's be honest, that British accent was pretty dreamy.

The second day on the job, Oliver brought with him a Thermos of hot tea. What's more British than that? He also used the word "brilliant" a lot. I'd say, "I'm going to go eat my lunch." And Oliver would exclaim, "Brilliant!" Oliver came to the store every day through the Thanksgiving break. He even volunteered to work overtime, telling Dad that he needed the money. But Arthur was convinced that Oliver wanted the OT just so he could spend more time with me. Arthur kept close tabs on us, asking me for updates at the end of each day. Honestly, I felt all along that Oliver was way out of my league, but Arthur—my coach and trainer—was always ready with a pep talk.

On the last day of inventory, a Saturday, Dad was running a little late. So, Oliver and the other students—along with Arthur—were waiting in the parking lot until Dad arrived to give out instructions. That's when Arthur heard it. It was Oliver. And he was talking to another student about one of his classes. There was absolutely no sign of a British accent. In fact, Oliver sounded exactly like every other farm kid in the Midwest. Stunned, Arthur turned to a student next to him and asked, "Remind me again where Oliver is from?" The answer: Indiana.

Being an out-of-state student who stuck close to campus, Oliver enjoyed anonymity among us townspeople. Since he had very little interaction with us, he could get away with his little charade.

I got to the store with Dad, and Arthur was standing by the coffee pot, just fuming.

"We have been hoodwinked," he declared. "We fell for the whole British act!"

To Arthur, the "total package" was now a "total loser." It didn't really matter to me at that point. It was the last day of inventory, and I knew I would never see Oliver again. But even today, I can't decide who was more disappointed, me or Arthur.

8.
COST CUTTING

My dad gave himself a paycheck every week for all of his hard work. Mom's paycheck was a microwave oven.

Not only did my parents run their businesses differently, they compensated themselves differently too. My mother didn't pay herself a salary in the traditional sense. Instead, she dipped into her business account for things like our school supplies, church giving, and doctor bills. She also covered big-ticket expenditures, such as costly auto repairs, a new roof and appliances—ergo the microwave.

Once when Mom came home from the store, she asked my father to carry in a giant box from the back seat of her car. When I saw it, I peppered her with questions.

"Is it a window air conditioner?"

"No."

"Is it a record player?"

"No."

"Is it a piece of furniture?"

"No. But here's a hint. It has something to do with tonight's supper."

When Dad cut open the box, I saw booklets at the top that said "Owner's Manual" and "Microwave Oven." I had seen ads for these ovens on TV, but none of my friends' parents had one yet—microwaves were both somewhat new to the scene and relatively expensive. While Dad took the packaging off the microwave, I cleared off a large space on the counter. Then, I asked Mom what she was going to make in the microwave.

"I'm going to heat up the bread," she said.

She picked up a loaf of Wonder bread and put it in the microwave—plastic bag and all. But first she slightly loosened the twist tie at the top. "If the bag is sealed too tightly, it might explode," she explained. According to Mom, a whole loaf of bread took only 10 to 15 seconds until it was fully warmed. She turned the TIME dial to 15 and pressed START. Then, Mom, Dad and I hovered in front of the door to watch the magic. After about 8 seconds, the bag caught on fire.

"Do flames mean that the microwave is working?" I asked.

There was no response from my parents. The bag had completely melted onto the bread as well as the bottom of the microwave. Mom stopped the oven and opened the door—acrid smoke spilled out. With tongs, she tugged at the molten mess, and that's when Dad spotted the problem. The bread bag's twist tie had a metal wire in it, and it got so hot that the paper that covered the wire caught on fire. The melted bread-bag essentially bonded at the molecular level with the bottom of the microwave, ruining it.

Once again, in the spirit of being helpful, I said to my parents, "Maybe next time you should read the owner's manual first." And once again, Mom and Dad turned and looked at me, and I saw those little icy daggers shooting out of their eyes.

Without saying a word, Dad unplugged the microwave and packed it back into the box. "Well," Mom said, "I'll just have to get another one."

Unlike my mother, my father paid himself a fixed salary, and his weekly paycheck was deposited in a joint checking account that my parents used for groceries, utility bills, and other day-to-day household expenses.

One day I got home from the stores early and found an envelope from the bank among the letters in our mailbox. When Mom opened it, she told Dad that their joint checking account was overdrawn. Apparently, my father hadn't gotten around to depositing his paycheck. It happened again a few weeks later. When Mom confronted Dad, he admitted that he wasn't depositing all of his weekly paychecks—that he needed that money to make payroll for his employees.

Over the ensuing months, the joint account was overdrawn several times. The bank covered the overdrafts, so none of the check recipients knew that the account had insufficient funds. But my parents faced a $25 fee for every check the bank had to cover.

It wasn't hard to figure out what was happening. I could see for myself that business at Dad's store had slowed significantly—especially during the summer harvest season. Farmers were struggling, and this time, bad weather and natural pests weren't the culprits. Geopolitical forces were choking the lifeblood out of McPherson's agricultural base.

One force at play was the cost of fuel. The OPEC oil embargo of 1973-'74 at one point jacked up global crude oil prices by 300%.[1] Another oil crisis hit in 1979 in the wake of the Iranian Revolution. Then in 1980, the Iran-Iraq war led to reductions in oil production, triggering fuel shortages that led to high prices and long lines at gas stations. Farmers' production costs skyrocketed, which in turn steeply cut into their profits—if there were any.

High prices for fuel and other consumer goods drove up inflation, meaning the dollar had less purchasing power. The rate of inflation rose 14.8% in 1980 over the previous year[2], a punishing increase for all American consumers, not just farmers. To curb inflation, the Federal Reserve increased the prime lending rate to a staggeringly high 21.5% in December 1980,[3] making it unaffordable for both businesses and individuals to borrow money and/or make their monthly debt payments.

As if farmers didn't have enough money problems, the U.S. enacted a grain embargo in 1980 as a response to the Soviet Union's invasion of Afghanistan. President Jimmy Carter canceled 17 million metric tons of *existing* wheat, corn, and soybean contracts, according to U.S. Wheat Associates, a trade group.[4] That grain had already been grown, and now it had no place to go. The bottom fell out of the grain market, despite government efforts to artificially stabilize prices. In much of the country, farmers risked paying more money to grow their crops than they were getting back when they sold them.

All of these events took their toll on America's farmers. Real farm income across the U.S. went from $22.8 billion in 1980 to $8.2 billion in 1983, according to an analysis by the Federal Deposit Insurance Corp.[5] During the recession that started in the early 1980s, over 3% of the country's 2.4 million farmers were quitting each year, by one estimate.[6]

Small businesses throughout McPherson County were reeling from the recession, leading many of them to lay off employees. That was reflected in the U.S. unemployment rate, which reached 10.8% at the end of 1982.[7]

It's important to understand these economic dynamics because what hurts farmers, hurts everyone else, especially in small towns like McPherson that rely on agriculture. I could see how this domino effect was impacting Copeland Supply, putting its long-term survival in doubt.

The first blows came in the mail. Along with the invoices and bills would be bankruptcy notices from some of Dad's customers. The notices are sent out by the court to all creditors and say that attempts at collecting on debts must stop. Usually, my dad had to write off these customers' debts as a total loss.

Instead of filing for bankruptcy, other customers bartered goods and services to pay down their account balances. From one cattleman, Dad accepted freezer-ready cuts of beef. Another customer gave my father a truckload of remains from a defunct golf-cart parts factory. Knowing how much Dad liked antique farm implements, one farmer brought in old tools and even a rusty old fire hydrant, which was gifted to our dog. He threw in a few Dillons sacks of freshly picked corn too.

When someone couldn't pay the bill, Dad would let it slide a month or so. My father didn't play hardball to collect on debts, mainly because compelling a farmer to pay up "would be like drawing blood from a turnip," he said.

Eventually, Dad turned to the bank and refinanced the loan on his building, mainly to pay his wholesale suppliers and cover his overhead expenses.

To be clear, my family had plenty to eat and clothes to wear, but the banker told my father more than once, "Don't be surprised when one morning you'll get to the store and find a padlock on the door." It never happened, but I know there were many sleepless nights.

Even then, it was obvious to Dad that he would have to take further action. That boiled down to two things: cutting costs and improving efficiency.

My father employed 10 or so full-time workers and subsidized their health insurance. Dad took fewer paychecks for himself so he could pay his employees. About this time, Jenny was offered a good job at a local plastics-extrusion plant. Losing her was a real blow to the store because she really knew the merchandise and the customers liked her.

"The invoices are kept in a binder under the freight desk," Jenny told my father on her last day at work. "And you'll find three months' of old timecards in the cabinet under the timeclock if there are any payroll questions."

Then Jenny turned to me. "The plants in the front window are watered every week," she said. "But the cactus behind the counter gets just a sip every other week."

If Dad was the brains of the store, Jenny was the heart that kept it going. Losing her was going to be an adjustment for everyone.

Not long after Jenny left, Heyfae decided to leave Dad's store too. I don't know the exact reason, but I suspect it was to help her husband, Norman, manage some car washes they owned. Heyfae always spoke lovingly about her husband, perhaps because they had gone through so much together. Norman was born and raised Mennonite, and Heyfae was non-Mennonite, what are called "people of the world." Their marriage led to his expulsion from the church, causing a painful rift in his family. Whenever Heyfae went to her in-laws, she could sit at the dining table to eat because she was a guest. But her husband had to eat on the back porch, so there were a lot of bitter feelings.

With Jenny and Heyfae gone, Dad desperately needed help on the sales floor. So, he called Ricky to see if he would come and work for him. It was a big risk, for sure, because their relationship could be volatile.

My brother had done well in military school, earning good grades and excelling on the wrestling team. But on the same day he got his diploma, Ricky and some fellow graduates broke into a house and stole some beer. They were arrested and charged with a misdemeanor. After coming back to McPherson, Ricky's drinking was getting bad, as was his behavior. Dad told him to stop coming to the store because he was driving away the customers.

Some time had passed since then, and Ricky was now living with a girlfriend in a mobile home in town. For the first time, this was a serious relationship, not a one-night stand. And he had steady work at a shipping depot in Moundridge. Life was good for Ricky, and he didn't want to go back and work for Dad.

My father hired just one new salesclerk. I helped pick up the slack after school, but on Saturdays I was often out of town for high school debate and speech tournaments. For a couple of summers, though, I worked for Dad full time. And that's when I found true love.

It started when I was at the freight counter in the back of the bolt room. Whenever a shipment came in, all of the boxes were piled on top of and next to the freight counter. Every order included a printout that listed the items in the shipment, along with multiple pages of pre-printed price tags with "Copeland Supply" at the top. Box by box, I matched the merchandise with the order sheet to make sure it was the right item and the correct quantity. Then I applied a price sticker to each thing and threw it into a shopping cart, which was probably the same cart that Ricky and I pinched from Gibson's. When the cart was full, I rolled it around the store to restock the shelves.

At 10 a.m. and 3 p.m. every workday, the guys in the steel shop took their coffee break. It was a well-deserved respite from the constant standing, lifting, and bending that their jobs required. Equally important, the break area had heat and air conditioning—both of which the shop lacked. So, while the shop guys—George the Welder, Cookie, and whoever else was working for Dad at the time—took their break, I sat on my perch at the freight counter nearby. I started to notice a new face in the break area: Junior, who was George the Welder's son. Like his dad, Junior was a giant at 6-foot-4 compared to my 5-foot, 3-inch frame. He wasn't much of a talker, either. But just from observing, I could tell that Junior was very capable in both metal fabrication and in dealing with customers.

One day I was at the freight counter, checking in a shipment of bolts. This job went pretty quickly because the bolt prices are written on a single tag that's affixed to the front of the bin, rather than on each individual bolt. So, I was zipping through the order, loading up my shopping cart with boxes of bolts to shelve. This all took place while the shop guys were on their afternoon break. I didn't realize it, but Junior was watching me as I worked. While I was in an aisle shelving bolts, I felt a tap on my shoulder. I turned to look, and there was Junior towering over me. "It looks like you put the course bolts in with the fine ones," he said.

He was right! I had been inadvertently mixing bolts with one type of thread into bins of bolts that had a different kind of thread. I realized that I would have to return to each bin, pick out the misplaced bolts and re-shelve them correctly. Here's what caught me by surprise. Rather than return to the break area, Junior went with me, aisle by aisle, and helped me re-sort the bolts.

He's letting his Mountain Dew grow warm while he's helping me! I thought to myself.

After that, I conveniently found myself at the freight counter, hoping to say "hi" to the guys at the end of their coffee break. But really, I just wanted to say hi to Junior. This went on for quite awhile.

One day I was at the freight counter when the afternoon coffee break ended. All of the shop guys went back to work except for one, Junior.

"I was wondering if you'd like to drive around after work tonight?" he asked me.

"Drive around? Like, drag Main?" I asked. That seemed a little out of character for both of us. It was such a public display.

"I mean like go to Dairy Queen or something," he said.

It wasn't exactly the most polished date request, but Dairy Queen sounded a lot better than dragging Main.

Later, after we had been dating a few months, Junior told me he was reluctant to ask out "the boss's daughter." It hadn't occurred to me that us dating could put him in an awkward position with my dad if we had a falling out.

But we didn't have a falling out. I was in love with Junior, and it seemed like I had known him for years because he was so much like his father. Junior was a he-man, just like his dad. I once watched him getting ready to change the oil in his car. His first step was to lift the whole front end of the vehicle off the ground while he slid a drain pan underneath it with his foot.

Junior and his family lived pretty far out in the country in a tiny town called Canton, about 7 miles east of McPherson. His mom and dad had a farm there that was so remote, you couldn't see another house or even a tall grain silo for miles. They mainly cultivated crops, but the farm also had chickens and a large vegetable garden. Most of the year, George the Welder worked in Dad's steel shop, while his wife, Barbara, worked in the cafeteria at the high school in Canton. During the summer harvest, George and Junior were absent from the steel shop and worked full time at their farm.

Even though they were farmers, Junior and his family were less impacted by the economic turmoil than many other farm families at the time. Both George and Barbara had non-farm jobs in the off season, and they supplied some of their own food from their large vegetable garden and a flock of chickens. George was also smart about money. He carried little or no debt, and he closely tracked grain prices. So, for example, if he felt the price of wheat was going to increase, he would store part of his harvest in his grain silo and sell it later when he would see a higher profit.

One year my parents gave me permission to tag along with Junior and his family for two weeks during the wheat harvest. My job was to help Barbara make and serve three meals a day in the field while George, Junior, and another man cut wheat. Barbara was incredibly kind and soft-spoken, just like George and Junior. Barbara had a way of putting people at ease, and she knew by name all the school kids in Canton because of her lunchroom job. Interestingly, Barbara spoke with a slight lisp, the result of a lightning strike years earlier.

In the mornings, Barbara and I methodically organized all of the food in ice chests, which were loaded into the back of Barbara's car, along with a folding table. We parked on the edge of the field and set up breakfast, typically egg sandwiches. We all ate while standing or sitting on the tailgate of one of the guys' pickups. Afterward, the men headed out to harvest wheat while Barbara and I cleaned up. At lunch time, we'd use a CB radio to summon the guys back to Barbara's car for lunch—usually sandwiches, potato chips, and sliced tomatoes and cucumbers from Barbara's garden. The meal always ended with a dessert, such as cookies or brownies. We'd repeat this drill at suppertime.

There was a little free time between cleaning up after one meal and setting up for the next meal. Sometimes, Barbara and I would drive around looking for abandoned homesteads so we could dig for bottles.

Based on our hunches, we raked the ground and made shallow

holes with a hand spade. We stopped if our tools made a light "clink" when they hit something hard, and more often than not it was some kind of glass bottle or jar—for milk, medicine, alcohol, cold cream, poison, all kinds of things.

The labels had come off just from being in the ground so long. But most of them had raised lettering in the glass, so you knew what had been inside them. My favorites were the medicine bottles—things like Hall's Catarrh Cure, Dr. King's New Discovery for Coughs and Colds, Lydia Pinkham's Medicine, and Piso's Cure for Consumption. Even after all of these years, I have the bottles that I found and admire them from time to time.

Those two weeks spent with Junior's family changed me in so many ways. They gave me a better understanding of the risks farmers face whenever they plant their crops. Weather played a huge role in how and when the wheat was harvested. I also learned that weather greatly affected the grain itself. Every load taken to a grain elevator was tested with a meter to determine its internal moisture content. Too much water meant the grain had to be dried or aerated to bring the moisture level down. The farmer got dinged for that extra step, earning less money per bushel than for loads with an acceptable moisture content.

Harvest was both exhilarating and exhausting for Junior's family. Much of their livelihood depended on their crops. In addition to wheat, they cultivated soybeans and sorghum, a grain used in animal feed. The family worked seamlessly as a team, and if something went wrong, they would huddle to troubleshoot a solution. Theirs was a business—just like my parents' hardware stores. That's obvious to me now, but it was a revelation back then.

I loved Junior, and I also loved his parents, who treated me like a daughter. I sat with the family at Junior's high school graduation ceremony. He was one of seven students in his entire graduating class. On the weekends, we visited almost every little cafe and truck stop diner in Central Kansas, places that George somehow knew about. Going out to eat at these homey restaurants was a form of entertainment for us. Other times, we took inner tubes to a nearby lake, which was located inside a game preserve for buffalo. I remember floating blissfully on my tube one hot, sunny day while staring at these giant animals in the distance.

The farm itself held a special place in my heart. I don't know how many acres the family owned—it is considered rude to ask a farmer that question. During the day, it felt like the farmhouse and barn sat on a tiny island that was surrounded by oceans of cropland. At night, only one utility light by the driveway interrupted the darkness, so the sky was like a canvas of twinkling stars.

When Barbara gave me a beautiful quilt that she made for me as a Christmas present, I was beginning to feel like I had two families, Junior's and mine. Mom and Dad were incredibly fond of Junior too. They could see that he treated me with respect and tenderness.

What they couldn't see was that the farm was a far more peaceful place for me than my own house, which had lots of yelling because Karan was now refusing to come to work at the stores. The day she turned 16, she dropped out of school, and her time was spent hanging out with a pretty rough crowd—other teens who were just as disruptive and unruly as she was.

"You're going to have NICE friends, whether you LIKE THEM or not!" my Dad shouted at her.

What my father didn't understand was that Karan's rough friends were actually more accepting of her and treated her better than many of the so-called "good" kids did.

For Karan's birthday one year, Ronnie came home from college with a giant bake-and-eat pizza he had made at the pizzeria in Lawrence where he worked. The plan was that the whole family would have it for supper that night.

The house smelled great while the pizza baked, and Karan didn't say a word while I set the table and made a side salad. When the timer buzzed, Karan removed the pizza from the oven and put it back in the box it came in. Pizza in hand, Karan started walking toward the door.

"Where are you going?" Ronnie asked.

Karan opened the front door, and we saw a car waiting in the driveway. Over her shoulder, Karan said, "Out with my friends."

Dad also had his hands full back at the store, where he was inventing ways to make selling hardware more efficient. First, he wanted customers themselves to find the merchandise that they needed. Second, he wanted to speed up the checkout process, especially since he had one fewer salesclerk. He came up with two ideas to make the business more cost effective—but only one of them worked.

His first idea was inspired by his service in the military. The bolt room had wall-to-wall drawers, bins and shelving units—so much stuff that it was difficult for customers to find anything without help. A bus system he saw as a serviceman in the South inspired him to try a new "mapping" system.

Apparently in the 1950s, a lot of the locals in this military town used the bus system to get around. But at the time, Dad said, many of them didn't know how to read. Because of this, it didn't make sense for the city to print signs that spelled out the stops and final destinations. Instead, the bus routes and stops were somehow designated using color-coded lines and three-dimensional geometric shapes. So, for example, someone who needed to find the nearest grocery store would be told, "Take the red line three stops to an orange cone," or some such.

Using a commercial-grade floor paint, Dad applied about a half-dozen solid and dotted lines in different colors on the floor. They all started at the front checkout counter, then fanned out in the bolt room. A variety of 3-D shapes, which were also color coded, went at the end of each shelving unit. The stripes and shapes gave the store a cool carnival vibe.

Dad wanted to try out his system before he taught it to me or the new hardware clerk. His guinea pig was a customer who came in asking for castle nuts. My father instructed him, "Follow the yellow line to the green sphere and turn left. Walk toward the red cube, and the castle nuts are on the right-hand shelf toward the bottom." The customer was so flummoxed by the complicated instructions that he just stood there. Since I already knew where the castle nuts were located, I led the customer to them. My father was undaunted, thinking that over time, customers would learn the system, and navigating the bolt room would become second nature to them.

In truth, I struggled with the system too. It's not that I didn't know where things were; I just couldn't articulate Dad's convoluted line-shape mapping system. Since the other clerk was still relatively new, she was completely at sea on both fronts— where things were located and how to navigate to them.

Dad was frustrated that his system wasn't catching on. Meanwhile, Arthur and the other coffee drinkers in the peanut gallery loved Dad's system. For them, it was great theater watching customers hopelessly wander around the aisles in search of cones, spheres, and cubes.

"Hey there, Bethy," they would hoot, "we got another puppy dog lost in the woods."

Eventually the concept died on the vine without anybody having to say the system was a flop.

Dad's next idea was also seen as a lark, but in truth, he was ahead of his time. It started with the purchase of a computer that was the size of an office desk. It stored data on doughnut-shaped discs that measured roughly 2-feet across. A low-resolution monitor was built into the computer's desk, and the letters and numbers on the black screen were formed with little green pixels. Hard copies of documents were made using a dot-matrix printer that taunted us with repeated paper jams. There was nothing plug-and-play about this machine and customizing it for Dad's store was far from intuitive. In another smart move, my father hired someone from Wichita who worked with computers to help him create systems for managing things like inventory, price sheets, and financial summaries.

It took weeks to set up the various functions and months for the bookkeeper to input all of the data. But slowly, it was making our lives easier. First, Dad created a "bolt binder" with printouts that listed the prices of hundreds of different types and sizes of bolts that he carried. Having that information at the counter saved us a trip to the bolt room to get the price from the bin tag. In the past, I sometimes wrote the various bolt and nut prices on my hand with a ballpoint pen so I would remember them when I got back to the front counter.

Next, he computerized the inventory in the steel shop. The shop binder broke down the prices of both metal that was sold by weight and metal that was sold by the linear foot. The price of labor also varied depending on the nature of the job, and the shop binder had that information too. Not only did this save us time, it reduced both clerical errors—such as writing down the wrong price—and math errors—such as undercharging for labor costs.

Over time, my father's system became more sophisticated, creating efficiencies in other ways. Before the computer, all of the fasteners were inventoried individually, with totals written down on a legal pad. In other words, tens of thousands of bolts, nuts, washers, and screws were counted by hand. To speed up the process, my father input every type of fastener he sold, along with the number of fasteners per pound. With the new system, the counters weighed all of the fasteners in a single bin. When the weight was input into the computer, the machine extrapolated the total number of pieces in stock. This approach easily cut in half the amount of time it took to inventory the store.

Next, my father used the computer for inventory management. The bookkeeper input all of the items that had been sold the previous day. Then once a week, the computer compiled a list of merchandise that was running low or out of stock. With that list, my father could order exactly what he needed from his suppliers with no more guessing.

The system wasn't perfect. First, when the computer was down, a technician from Wichita or Topeka had to drive to McPherson to service it. Second, it relied mainly on manually input data. Things like bar codes and hand scanners weren't widely used back then. And of course, nothing was connected to the internet, which was also in its infancy. Finally, I don't know what my father paid for the computer, but the upfront costs for the machine and the technical training must have been high. But the efficiencies it created easily covered his initial investment. For example, he used to send his accounts receivables to an outside company, which then printed monthly statements that were mailed to his customers. Now Dad could print statements on his own computer, which saved him a lot of money. Over time, computers became smaller, faster, and cheaper, making it easier for other small, independent stores like Mom and Dad's to digitize their inventories.

My father seized on one more cost-cutting measure that enabled him to buy hardware for far less than what he paid his suppliers. For years we had been going to an annual hardware show held at a convention center in Kansas City. On Saturday after the store closed, we would drive four hours from McPherson to Kansas City so we could attend the show all day Sunday.

My parents felt that Karan and I were too young to stay at home alone, so we went to Kansas City with them. At first the family stayed in a hotel with a swimming pool, which was great because it gave me and my sister something fun to do while Mom and Dad were at the convention hall.

And one year they dropped me and Karan off in Lawrence for the day, where Ronnie showed us around the KU campus. That night he took us to a song-and-dance revue put on by the school's fraternities and sororities. The "preppy" movement was going at full tilt, and my sister and I thought the men and women on stage were about the most beautiful people we had ever seen.

But eventually, my parents took my sister and me to the KC hardware shows in an old Dodge camper that my dad used sometimes when he went fishing. Mom would load it up with bedding and pre-made meals. It was probably done to save money, but at eight miles per gallon, the camper wasn't terribly cost effective. Dad would park the RV behind the convention hall, and a maintenance person usually let him run an extension cord from the camper to an electrical outlet on the outside of the building. That way we could run the air conditioner at night to stay cool.

Inside the convention hall, major manufacturers like Black and Decker (power tools), Stanley (hand tools), Philips (lighting), and Kwikset (door hardware) had booths touting their latest models and finishes. It wouldn't seem possible to make hardware look glitzy, but most of the booths had snazzy lights and slick displays.

One crowd-pleaser was a booth with assorted power tools designed for DIYers. There, two sexy women in bikini tops and short-shorts wore gun holsters around their waists. The women looked very much like the famed Dallas Cowboys' cheerleaders as they strutted around the booth with power drills in their holsters. When the exhibitor said "draw," the women pulled the drills out of the holsters and pretended to fire them in the crowd. The whole time they were smiling and winking at everyone.

There were product demos, including one in which a two-part epoxy was used to affix progressively heavier items to a piece of plywood. It started with a lightweight golf ball and ended with a metal step stool.

"It's impressive, but I'm not sure why anyone would want to glue a step stool to the wall," my father told the epoxy salesman.

And once an hour, there was a drawing for a door prize, which Karan and I always looked forward to. We both had a bunch of tickets that had been doled out to Mom and Dad when we first walked into the convention hall. My sister and I crowded around the announcer's table every time the numbers were called out on a loudspeaker. The funny thing is that every single prize was completely worthless to us, but we still got excited at each drawing.

Karan was far luckier than I was. Once she won a Schlage door handle and deadbolt set—which Mom later sold at her store. Another time when Karan's number was pulled, the announcer said she had won a golf cart. Karan and I went bananas over the prospect of whizzing around the neighborhood in the cart. That's when the announcer came forward with a golf cart that was pulled along behind the golfer, like it was a piece of luggage. We were crushed. Dad took the cart, thinking he could sell it at his store. But none of his customers seemed to want it, so the pull cart just gathered dust and cobwebs.

The very end of the hardware show is where my parents made their move. The exhibitors had hauled a lot of merchandise into the convention hall at the beginning of the show. But they didn't want to break down their booths and haul everything back with them at the end. So most everything on display in the booths was available to buy below its wholesale cost. The price also included any display racks and shelving. It was a way for my parents to buy merchandise at a lower price than what they were paying their hardware suppliers. This strategy likely saved them hundreds of dollars.

Dad at a hardware convention with Heyfae and Jenny,
his very capable salesclerks.

All four of us had to stick around until the very end of the show. Then, Mom and Dad bought whatever merchandise they wanted from the booths. We disassembled the display racks and shelves and hauled them—along with countless loads of hardware—out to the camper. By the time we were finished, it was well after 7 o'clock. The camper was so stuffed, there was very little space to sit for the long drive home.

The camper wasn't exactly a jack rabbit with the additional weight of the merchandise, so the trip lasted much longer than the four hours it would take to get there by car. We wouldn't arrive back in McPherson until well after midnight. When we got there, Dad first parked the camper in front of Mom's store, and we unloaded everything that she had bought into a storage area in the back. When that was done, Dad pulled the camper up to his store so we could unload everything he purchased at the freight counter in the bolt room. My parents wanted everything unloaded that night so as not to disrupt business during the day. Karan and I were exhausted at the end, but even so, we were expected to go to school on Monday.

As time passed, the local economy continued to flag, and a number of businesses closed for good. Among the casualties in downtown McPherson: the Duckwall's and Woolworth five-and-dime stores, an Otasco store, a Sears catalog storefront, and a cute gift shop called the Doll House. But nobody was counting out our small-but-mighty city. McPherson County had weathered the Great Depression, thanks to the discovery of oil in the 1920s. And after World War II, at the onset of farm consolidation, civic leaders had the foresight to develop a robust industrial base, including major manufacturers like Cargill, CertainTeed, and Johns Manville. This strong commercial tax base kept McPherson economically sound, while some other nearby cities became ghost towns. In fact, a lot of people from neighboring towns—like Galva, Lindsborg, Moundridge, and Inman—were driving back and forth to McPherson because it had more jobs.

Karan found work at a local plastics plant, a coveted position because it paid well and offered good benefits. This job required her to remove plastic pipe fittings as they came down a conveyer belt. She loaded the fittings onto a cart. And when it was full, she rolled it to a window and picked up an empty cart that she would then refill at the conveyer belt.

"I would rather plunge burning hot needles into my eyes," I told my sister.

But she loved this job. She made good money and liked the people she worked with. There were few demands in terms of interacting with customers and, most important, she wasn't under the thumbs of her mother and father. I was beginning to realize that Karan didn't have trouble with authority, she just had trouble with *parental* authority.

As for Mom's store, it could have easily succumbed to the recession. But her approach to business was both more conservative and more financially savvy than my father's. She continued with her promotions that drew customers to the store, and she shied away from unnecessary purchases, including a computer system like Dad's next door, especially since her store was much smaller. She also ran a lean household. Most of our meals were eaten at home, and any home improvements like new carpeting were put on hold.

Even so, some circumstances were outside of her control. While Christmas season was Mom's busiest time of year, the second busiest was wedding season, which typically ran from May through September. Engaged couples came to B&G Hardware to create a gift registry so guests could purchase exactly what they wanted for showers and the wedding day. Mom was the only one who was allowed to accompany the couple as they made their selections. She wrote each item down in a gift-registry book and specified details like model numbers, patterns, and preferred colors to make sure the bride and groom received just what they had hoped for. With some of the larger weddings, the list of housewares, appliances, and home decor went on for several pages. Like at Christmastime, their selections were gift wrapped for free, and Mom and I delivered the packages to people's homes after the store closed.

Pyrex dishes were popular picks among brides to be.

There was a particularly large wedding in town that was scheduled to take place on a Saturday at Lakeside Park, where a big tent and enough chairs to seat 100 people were set up. In the weeks leading up to the nuptials, Mom's customers had purchased almost everything listed on the bride and groom's gift registry. After closing time on the eve of the wedding, Mom drove me around town so I could drop off the last of the gifts purchased for the bride and groom. Tired but pleased, Mom was in a particularly good mood at the supper table that night, since this event likely was her most profitable wedding ever.

"Who wants ice cream?" Mom exclaimed after we were finished. In a rare treat, we went to Dairy Queen for a round of Blizzards.

On Sunday, the morning after the wedding, we were at home getting ready for church when the telephone rang. Mom answered it and frowned at what she heard. Then she walked to her bedroom to finish the call privately on the phone extension there. Along the way, she picked up her *Emily Post's Etiquette* book. She hollered from her bedroom for me to hang up the receiver in the kitchen. But instead, I listened in, careful to hold my hand over the mouthpiece.

"We were all sitting under the tent waiting for the ceremony to begin," the caller explained. "A vintage car pulled up, and the bride's father helped his daughter get out of it."

"Uh-huh," my mom said.

"Then, the bride's father took her arm and started walking into the tent, heading toward the altar," the caller continued. "But only the pastor was standing there—all by himself. The groom wasn't there!"

"Oh, no! That poor woman," Mom said.

"We sat around in those chairs, waiting and waiting for the groom to show up. Even the bride was sitting there with us. After a while, she started to cry. She was crying so hard that her makeup was running down the front of her gown—and it was such a lovely dress.

"So finally, the bride's mother took her hand and led her back to the car. Then they drove away. We were left just sitting there, not knowing what to do."

My mom didn't say anything, but I could sense that she was holding her breath.

"So, the question is, what do we do with all the gifts that we bought for the wedding?"

I heard Mom flipping through the well-worn pages of her etiquette book, and she summarized what she learned. "If the groom dies before the wedding, the bride gets to keep all of the presents," Mom said. "But if the wedding is called off, the couple should return the presents to the guests."

While I was listening in, I was whispering the story to my dad. After he heard what had happened, his usual frown deepened. After hanging up, Mom came out of the bedroom and looked ashen.

"Maybe the groom will change his mind?" Dad asked her hopefully.

"You're assuming she would take him back," she replied. "No, we're going to be busy next week with refunds on all of those presents."

This one episode likely cost her hundreds of dollars, making it a good lesson in the vicissitudes of owning a small business. So many factors—the weather, the harvest, the price of gas, and even a groom who gets cold feet—can unexpectedly cut deeply into the profits.

My parents weren't native Kansans, but they had come to personify the state's Latin motto: "Ad astra per aspera," which means, "Through hardships to the stars."

In truth, I think my mom worried about my father's finances more than my dad worried about his finances. At some point in her 50s, Mom took out a $100,000 life-insurance policy and told my dad to pay off the mortgage on his building after she died. It seemed unusual to me that Mom would be planning so far ahead, but now I realize that she wanted to ensure that Dad would be okay if something were to happen to her.

She either already knew that something was wrong, or she possessed an incredible power for prophesy.

9.
TURNING POINT

B ethy, come to the bedroom with me. I want to show you something," my mother said.

We had just finished supper, and the table hadn't been cleared yet.

It's odd Mom needs me for something before the dishwasher's been loaded, I thought to myself.

My parents' bedroom was in the back of the house, and when we got there, Mom closed the door. Unclear about what was happening, I merely stood there as my mother unbuttoned her blouse. Then, she lifted up her bra.

I had just completed my junior year in high school at the time, and I still had so much to learn about the world around me. But even to me, a teenager, I knew that when I looked at my mother's chest, what I saw was very bad. One of her nipples was so inverted, it almost reached the wall of her chest.

"Mom, I don't know what this is, but you need to see a doctor," I told her.

She was able to get an appointment with our family physician a few days later. After examining her, the doctor sent my mother to an oncology clinic for a mammogram. But I am almost certain that our doctor knew all along what he was looking at.

Hutchinson is located about a half-hour southwest of McPherson, and the road between the two towns was a two-lane highway. Mom told my father that she would be fine driving herself to the oncologist. I was at school when Mom got her mammogram, but she later described to me the giant machine in a darkened room used to take images of her breast.

"Bethy, I was told to stand perfectly still, and the machine

143

smashed each boob flat while it took a picture."

"Did it hurt?" I asked.

"You better believe it hurt," she said.

As Mom awaited the results of the mammogram, we pondered that menacing machine. My theory was that the people who designed it—most likely men—never actually had it used on them personally. That led my mother to ask, "If men had to get routine mammograms, how would they have designed the machines for use on themselves?"

After some thought, I replied, "It would involve resting their boobs lightly on a heated Nerf ball."

Even before an official diagnosis, the situation seemed grave. Still, Mom told my father that it was too early to start worrying.

But the diagnosis was inevitable: Mom had an advanced case of breast cancer, becoming one more statistic in an alarming trend. Breast cancer incidence jumped 32% between 1980 and 1987, according to data from the National Cancer Institute. (Part of that increase is attributed to the growing use of mammography to detect breast disease.)[8]

When Mom got home from Hutchinson, she made sure to tell each family member the news herself, even if it was just over the phone. We had lots of questions, of course, but it was too early to know any answers.

We didn't know anybody in McPherson who had been treated for breast cancer, so this was all new to us. But Mom said the waiting room in Hutch was full of women—many with wigs and head scarves—who were there to see an oncologist.

One thing Mom made clear: No one outside the family could be told about the cancer diagnosis. She didn't want people feeling sorry for her, I'm sure, but I also think she was striving for "business as usual" at B&G Hardware.

The next step was major surgery, and it was scheduled at McPherson's Memorial Hospital almost immediately. When filling out the admissions paperwork, my mother indicated on one of the forms that she didn't want her name released to the newspaper or radio station. Even if just one person heard or read that Mom was in the hospital, everybody else in town would know it before the sun went down that day.

My mother underwent a radical mastectomy, which was performed by a local surgeon, whom we all knew well. My father sat in the surgical waiting room, along with two of his siblings, Harold and Tootsie, who had come up from Texas. A woman on staff was on hand to act as a liaison to the operating room. Dad nervously talked about everything and nothing, just to pass the time.

Finally, after several hours, Mom's surgeon came to the waiting room to say that her mastectomy had been completed. She was in the recovery room, after which she would be taken to her room on the hospital's third floor. Then the surgeon gave all three of them—my dad, his brother, and his sister—a rundown on how the operation went. Depending on the listener, the surgeon said he was able to:

> a) Remove all of the cancer.
> b) Remove most of the cancer.
> c) Remove the cancer in the breast but not in other areas.

After school, I went to Mom's hospital room and was there when she came up from the recovery room. She was incredibly groggy and said very little. After giving Mom a peck on the cheek, Dad said we should leave and let her get some rest. The surgeon said he expected Mom to be in the hospital for four or five days.

After classes the next day I went straight to the hospital to sit and keep Mom company. I could tell that she was in pain because she asked for medication. That was a surprise because she had such a fear of drug addiction.

I can't remember what we talked about while she lay in bed. I recall reading Ann Landers' advice column to her from the newspaper. I updated her on what was going on at the stores and at home. (Mom's part-time clerks were working full time until Mom was ready to return.) I also did my homework while my mother dozed. She was notorious for her loud snoring, and this was no different. When she woke, I teased her that the other patients were complaining about a "chainsaw noise."

It was very much the same routine on the second day, but she didn't sleep as much. That afternoon, we could see a candy striper in the hallway outside Mom's room. Candy stripers were high school students who volunteered to help the nursing staff with things like making beds and delivering meal trays to patients' rooms. In peering down the hallway, Mom and I could see that the candy striper was struggling to push some sort of cart. It looked so overloaded, we were afraid that it was going to tip over.

As the candy striper got closer to Mom's room, we could see that the cart was overflowing with plants and flowers—so many, in fact, that it was difficult for the girl to see over them and steer the cart. She came to a stop outside of my mother's room and lightly rapped on the door. It was hard to miss the cart, with all the flowers crammed on it. My mother said to the candy striper, "Goodness! Is one of those for me?"

And the candy striper said, "They're ALL for you."

I was so touched that I started to cry. Despite my mother's efforts to keep her hospitalization a secret, word somehow got out. And it felt like the whole town of McPherson was pointing a firehose full of love directly at my mother. It happened again the next day and the day after with the candy striper and her cart.

She got a bouquet of pink sweetheart roses from Tootsie and a large potted houseplant from her employees at the store. June, her hairdresser, sent a nosegay of posies, and Bob and Lois from the fried-chicken restaurant sent flowers with a happy face helium balloon attached to the vase. Junior, George, and Barbara sent an arrangement of vibrant sunflowers. And, aptly so, the women's group at church sent a prayer plant. A handful of her longtime customers—even ones who seldom came in—sent flowers and plants. And the coffee drinkers in the peanut gallery all signed a get-well card and mailed it to the hospital. It showed a puppy with the words: "Sit. Stay. Heal."

By the time of her dismissal, the walls of Mom's room were lined three deep with vases of flowers and potted plants.

She went back to the store the day after she got home from the hospital. I joined her at the store after school to help out until closing time. She mainly stayed in the office, but customers popped their heads in to say "hi" all day long. Mom had to heal from the surgery before there could be any talk of chemotherapy or radiation, and she said that working was a good distraction. Eventually, however, she learned her fate from the oncologist. She would have six months of chemotherapy once a week, followed by six weeks of radiation five days a week.

Up until then, Mom didn't know anyone in town with breast cancer. But when she got out of the hospital, a number of women—some of whom she didn't know—stopped by the store. They had gone through—or were still going through—the same ordeal. It was a somewhat silent sisterhood back then, long before the pink ribbons and 1-in-9 awareness campaigns seen today. These women were blunt about what Mom was facing. But they also wanted to encourage her.

"It's like riding a Brahman bull in a rodeo," one told her. "You stay on for eight difficult seconds, and then it's over and you go on with your life."

Treating women with breast cancer was much different 40 years ago. Surgery tended to be more invasive, with many women opting for mastectomies, in which the breast is removed, over lumpectomies, in which a portion of breast tissue is removed. There were fewer choices among chemotherapy medications, and many of them were known to kill patients' healthy cells in addition to attacking tumors. And women's quality of life was also far worse, since fewer anti-nausea drugs were available back then.

My mother was no different. Lois, her dear friend, went with Mom to her first treatment in Hutchinson. Including a consultation with the oncologist, some blood work, and the chemo infusion, Mom and Lois were at the clinic for several hours. The side effects kicked in shortly after Mom got back to the store—extreme fatigue and difficulty keeping food down. Lois must have seen what was happening, because she and some other women developed a rotation schedule of driving Mom to her weekly treatments. The women kept car-sickness bags and washcloths in the car for my mother.

All of the trips went smoothly, except for one. A friend named Dorothy happened to be driving Mom that day, and they were on the two-lane highway coming back to McPherson. The sky looked threatening, and the radio said the county was under a tornado watch. Dorothy and Mom saw what looked like a funnel cloud forming in the distance. Dorothy made the quick decision to find a place for them to shelter.

She saw a road running perpendicular to the highway just ahead, and she turned off the highway. The safest place they decided, was a farmhouse down the road. When they got to the house, Dorothy ran up to the door and rang the bell. It was likely that the couple inside was already hunkered down in their basement listening to the latest weather reports on the radio. Nonetheless, a man answered the door. Dorothy explained the situation—my mother was feeling quite ill, and it looked like a tornado was forming up ahead. Could they please stay there until it passed?

Apparently, the man's wife overheard the conversation, and without hesitating, she and her husband sprang into action. Under skies that were an ominous gray-green hue, the woman and Dorothy helped my mother out of the car and into the house. Winds whipping, the man drove Dorothy's car into a garage-shed on his property.

Once the four of them got settled in the basement, they introduced themselves. That's when the woman exclaimed, "I know you!" gesturing toward my mother. It was one of Mom's customers. And apparently my mother had once put in a special order for a replacement part the woman needed for her vacuum cleaner. Somehow, talking about her vacuum and other trips to Mom's store eased some of the tension in the room. In just over an hour, the weatherman said the skies over McPherson County were beginning to clear as the storm moved toward the east.

They emerged from the house to see scattered limbs and toppled patio furniture, but no lasting damage. Dorothy and Mom thanked their impromptu hosts and went on their way to McPherson.

Early on in her treatment regimen, Mom was strong enough to manage both her store and the household. But after each infusion, she felt increasingly worse. That's when what I call "the miracle of McPherson" started to unfold. All of those people whom my mom had helped in the past came forward to sustain her through the treatment regimen.

"Bake this for 30 minutes at 350 degrees," one customer told Mom when dropping off a casserole at closing time.

"I left a platter of deli meat and cheeses on your kitchen counter," another Main Street merchant called to say one day.

With each treatment, however, our friends and neighbors came up with more ways to help out. And even the small acts of kindness had a huge impact.

"The freight is here," George the Welder told my mother on his way to the delivery bay at the back of her store. "Once it's unloaded and checked off, I'll send the driver up so you can sign the paperwork."

He and Junior had been coming over from Dad's store to unload her weekly deliveries. The door to her delivery bay was incredibly heavy and had to be hoisted with a chain on a pulley. Lifting it was much easier for Junior than it was for my Mom.

Whenever Mom called in a refill for a prescription, the druggist would deliver it to her in person at her store.

"Larry, you shouldn't go to the trouble," Mom protested. "I could have picked that up."

"It's nothing, Betty," he replied. "In fact, it's on my way home."

Once Mom started losing her hair, June, her beloved stylist gave her a call.

"Betty, I have a wig and a backup wig ready for you to try on," she said. "When can you come to the shop?"

Once the wigs were fitted at the salon, June would drop by the store to pick up one or the other when it needed to be re-styled. Then, if time permitted, June lingered in Mom's office for a cup of coffee and a cigarette—just like in the old days at the salon.

Our church family helped in countless ways. Even the youth group jumped in with an occasional "rake and run." They descended on our yard en masse to collect all the leaves, stacking the bags on the curb for pickup.

One day, we arrived home after closing time to find that the house was spotless. The kitchen, living room, and dining room were sparkling, and so were the bathrooms.

"I hadn't realized how dirty things had gotten until they had been cleaned," Mom said. "I wonder who did this?"

Next to the phone was a note from my sister. All it said was: "I want to help out. Karan."

My sister was living on her own by that time in a mobile home on the east end of town. She had to quit her job at the plastics plant because the repetitive nature of loading the cart gave her carpal-tunnel syndrome and required surgery.

Now she was a cashier at a storefront with three businesses inside: dry cleaner, liquor store, and bait shop. When somebody walked through the door, she didn't know if she'd be selling single-malt scotch or live earthworms.

She didn't have much contact with the family, but every couple of weeks, we would come home and find that she had cleaned the house.

Mom made it through six miserable months of chemotherapy. Always a fighter, she said she was down but not out. All throughout, I don't think she missed a day at the store, even if it was just for a few hours. She now faced the next hurdle: six weeks of radiation therapy, five days a week. Not only was the treatment regimen grueling, she had to endure 60 more trips to and from Hutchinson and McPherson. Again, her friends came up with a schedule to drive Mom to the clinic.

There were side effects with the radiation, but the worst was the fatigue.

"It's like I need a crane to pull me out of bed in the morning," Mom told me.

The Christmas holidays were coming up, and she wasn't sure she could handle keeping the store open until 8:30 p.m. every night, plus a half day on Sunday. That's when another remarkable dynamic unfolded. When the store got busy with a lot of customers, or if her employee had gone home for the day, customers started helping other customers find the merchandise. Many of Mom's regulars were just as familiar with the store as she was. They would jump in to help someone locate what they needed, then write up a sales ticket, with tax included in the total. A carbon copy of the ticket and the customer's payment were placed next to the cash register for Mom to ring up later.

Separately, my mother had another Christmas tradition, but because of the radiation, she had decided to skip it that year.

Since what seemed like forever, my mother had made dozens of dozens of cookies to take to our neighbors and friends around town. She would also make a big platter with an assortment of cookies to take to the store for her customers. Missing a year of baking cookies didn't seem like a big deal to me at first. Then I remembered Mom's mantra:

"First and foremost, 'God is love,' but 'Food is love' is a close second."

One evening the phone rang at home, and I answered it. On

the line was the woman from the hospital who coordinated the volunteers—including the candy stripers who had delivered mountains of flowers to Mom when she had her surgery. The coordinator said that some of the volunteers had volunteered to help Mom make her Christmas cookies. They would be coming over the following week to start baking.

With so many people helping her, Mom wanted to do something that would dramatically help herself: stop smoking. I was thrilled—quitting was something I had been urging her to do for years.

It started when Mom saw an ad in the McPherson Sentinel saying that a smoking-cessation program was coming to town. It consisted of a week-long series of seminars in a hotel banquet room. There, hypnosis would be used to help Mom and other smokers kick the habit. She signed up for hypnotherapy because her earlier efforts to go cold turkey had failed.

After the first night, Mom came home with several cassette tapes, which she was supposed to listen to, reinforcing her hypnotherapy. The smokers were instructed to cut back on the number of cigarettes they had each day, and to listen to the cassettes at bedtime each night. They were also given a form to carry everywhere they went. Whenever Mom felt the urge for a cigarette, she had to write down on the form the date and time it happened. Next to it was a box for her to fill in: What was the first thought that came to your mind when this craving struck? The idea was that if smokers could identify their "triggers," they could figure out ways to avoid or overcome them.

I wanted to be supportive and encouraging to my mother, just like she was to my father when he quit smoking before I was born. So, I put little dishes of hard candy around the house, thinking the sweets would help curb her urges. Mom did great, slowly reducing her daily cigarette intake from a pack a day all the way down to zero. I was so proud of her, especially since she was simultaneously enduring radiation. On the evenings that Mom took out the cards for a hand of solitaire, I would jump in and offer to play Spades with her instead. That would keep her hands occupied while hopefully reducing some of the cravings. At bedtime, she listened to her cassette tapes. To me, she was a model student.

This went on for a couple of months. Until, that is, I came home one day and found her sitting at her place at the end of the supper table, smoking a cigarette. She looked discouraged but resigned to her lapse. Thankfully, I had enough maturity by that time not to nag or scold her. Who am I to judge? But I did ask my mother, "What is it that made you break down?"

That's when Mom handed me the form that the hypnotist had handed out, the one with the first thought that came to her mind when she craved a cigarette. It looked like this:

> "Bethy won't know."
> "Bethy won't know."
> "Bethy won't know."
> "Bethy won't know."
> "Bethy won't know."
> "Bethy won't know."
> "Bethy won't know."

I went from feeling disappointed in my mother to feeling disappointed in myself. I must have been putting a tremendous amount of pressure on her to quit. I realized that she was making the effort more for me than for herself. She had enough on her plate right now and didn't need me telling her something she already knew.

"Mom, I'm so sorry. I'm such a jerk," I said. "I just want the cancer to be gone. I'm not going to worry about the other stuff, okay?"

"My treatment is almost over," she said. "And don't apologize. I've been through a lot worse."

10.
THE SUMMER OF 1937

Her parents christened her Grace Elizabeth when she was born in Winslow, Arizona, in 1931. Her brother, Jim, was born three-and-a-half years later.

Mom didn't talk much about her childhood. In fact, she possessed very few memories whatsoever of growing up, like she had a big blank spot in her brain. On the few occasions that she shared any recollections—and only because I prodded—I felt my heart aching for her.

My mom's father, John, supervised crews that built roads and dams, mainly in Arizona and New Mexico. John and his wife, Villa Claude, moved the family from place to place to work on road projects, living in a tent at each job site. It was a dusty, nomadic existence, but Mom always thought her family was "rich" because their tent had a wooden floor—not just dirt—and because her parents owned a car.

On a blistering hot day in 1937, John and his crew were working on a road project in a canyon just outside of Globe, Arizona. Located in the Sonoran Desert, Globe bakes in summertime temperatures that can reach as high as 118 degrees. Periodically, this hot air interacts with cool, moist air in the atmosphere, resulting in violent thunderstorms. The desert's parched, sandy earth can't absorb a sudden influx of water, leading to flooding that makes driving extremely dangerous.

On August 12, Villa Claude, along with five-year-old Betty and two-year-old Jim, were in a car on their way to pick John up at the end of his workday. A flash flood struck, taking everybody by surprise. John and some other workers reported seeing an 18-foot wall of water topped by two feet of hail and ice sweep the car toward an embankment—with Villa Claude and the children still inside.

Nearby, a bulldozer operator saw what was happening and tried to position the dozer in front of the car as it tipped over the side of the embankment. With flood waters rising, John managed to pull Betty out of the car. When they got to higher ground, she turned back to look. That's when she saw her mother slumped over the wheel of the car, drowned with a broken neck at age 36.

Meanwhile, her little brother had been ejected from the car as it pitched over the embankment. Floodwaters carried the toddler roughly two-and-a-half miles farther down into the canyon. A Native American man walking across a railroad trestle spotted something bouncing along in the current and realized that it was a small child. He laid down on the trestle and grabbed Jim by his clothing as the waters swept him along. Once Jim was pulled to safety, the Native American didn't know what to do with him. So, this Good Samaritan took Jim to the sheriff's office in Miami, Arizona, and from there, he was transferred to a hospital.

The next thing Betty remembered was seeing her mother laid out in a coffin that had been placed in someone's living room, likely Villa Claude's parents' home. That night, my mom went outside and looked up at the stars. Then, she asked God to bring her mother back to life so they could be together again.

What happens next is fuzzy, with lots of gaps, because both Betty and Jim erased many childhood memories from their minds.

After her mother's death, Betty went to live with her grandparents—Villa Claude's parents—in Deming, New Mexico. Jim went with his father to another job in Arizona, in a town known today as Sierra Vista. They lived in a tent, and John hired a woman to care for young Jim while he was at work. During this time, someone in the tent camp reported that Jim was being abused. One day, when John came back to the tent from work, the little boy was gone. John discovered that Jim's grandparents had come and taken the boy with them back to Deming.

As children, Betty and Jim both recalled that they were frequently separated, sometimes unsure of where the other sibling was living. For a time, however, they stayed with their grandparents in Deming and in Lordsburg, New Mexico. At one point, the four of them lived in a house owned by Betty and Jim's uncle, who also operated a 14-room motel. Apparently, the uncle was well off, but he had children of his own and resented having to also take care of his parents and his sister's two children.

Jim recalls his uncle sending him out to gather firewood. While he was out, the uncle gave his own children candy so he wouldn't have to share any with young Jim. It was a small injustice, but one that even when he was 90 years old, Jim said he could never forget.

When money was especially tight, Betty and her little brother bore the brunt of the suffering. Fortunately, another uncle drove a "welfare truck" that provided occasional food and other charitable support to needy families, Jim recounted years later. "Without that truck, we would have very possibly gone hungry," he added.

Reluctant to give details because they were difficult to relive, both Betty and Jim said that their well-to-do uncle and their grandfather were both incredibly harsh. Jim remembered their grandmother walking mile and a half each way to do the motel's laundry—and she wasn't given any food or money for lunch. Jim's job was to steady the pole that held up the clothesline. "Heaven forbid, I let those clothes touch the ground," he said.

Betty recounted that she once climbed up the base of a windmill to avoid her grandfather, who was chasing her with a leather razor strop.

"Everyone in that family disliked Betty," Jim said. "I have no idea why. She was just a little girl."

Schooling was sporadic. After a long, unexplained absence from elementary school, Betty shaved her eyebrows off before returning to the classroom in hopes her teacher would assume that she had been gravely ill. It must have worked. After taking her seat, Betty said the teacher took one look at her and didn't ask a single question.

Eventually, Betty fled her grandparents' home. Most likely, that was in the eighth grade, when her schooling ended. Shortly after, she got a job at a truck stop and cafe called White's Camp, located 9 miles west of Lordsburg. Betty fondly recalled that the owners, Hubert and Nora, willingly took her in and gave her work. Even so, money was scarce for them too. Not only was the world at war, but Hubert and Nora had to support their eight children who had lived past infancy. Betty grew close with the family, and Nora became sort of a foster mother to her.

In 1947, two weeks after her 16th birthday, Betty married Nora and Hubert's third-oldest child, Roy. Within six months, Betty became pregnant. In December 1948, Betty and Roy had a baby boy, whom they named Lawrence—Larry for short. Roy worked for his parents, then went on to become a port inspector in Hidalgo County, New Mexico. Of Roy and Betty's marriage and home life, very little was said.

Years later, the most Betty would reveal was that Roy was a chronic alcoholic. For reasons known only to her, Betty once again fled her home—this time leaving behind her husband and baby boy. Nora and Hubert took over raising Larry, by then a toddler, and kept him for many of his formative years.

Betty and her brother Jim had loosely stayed in touch, and Jim was able to provide some details. After Betty and Roy divorced, Betty left Lordsburg to work briefly as a waitress in Page, Arizona, where construction was set to begin on the Glen Canyon Dam. She was doing well enough to buy a car, "but unfortunately she rolled it one night" in an accident, Jim said. Soon after, Betty married a second time. Jim couldn't remember the man's name, only that he was Hispanic and "had a bum leg." This marriage must have been just as unhappy as the first one, because it, too, was brief.

In the early 1950s, Betty ended up in Gallup, New Mexico,

and got a job at the famed El Rancho Hotel. A hard worker and quick learner, Betty would probably do well here, but it would take time. For the near future, she would be waiting tables and tending bar. She had no family nearby and mostly kept to herself at work.

So here she was, in her early 20s. Twice married and divorced. And the mother of a son that she had left behind.

Then one day, Gene Copeland walked in the door, sent to Gallup to work on an oilfield project. Little did he or Betty Carey know that their lives would soon change for the better.

I had so many questions about my mother's past, but whenever I asked more about her background, she never wanted to talk about it. Too much pain. And too much shame, perhaps.

In researching this book, I reconnected with Mom's brother Jim, my uncle, many years after her death. He is now 90 years old and coincidentally lives near my Aunt Tootsie in East Texas. She and I drove there to visit him one afternoon in the spring, when the fields near his home were awash in blue bonnets.

Back in the 1940s, Jim had known my mother's first husband, Roy. He also knew about her second marriage. That one came as a surprise to me, and I'm not even sure that my father knew that she had been married and divorced a second time before they met.

"Why would Mom wed so soon after enduring such a painful marriage to Roy, her first husband?" I asked Jim.

"I cannot imagine being a young female in that era," he explained. "Almost everyone was poor. Women had very few employment opportunities at the time, and without an education, it would have been almost impossible to survive without a man."

Then he added this, which haunts me even today: "Betty had to rear herself," Jim said. "I had it better than she did, and I promise you that my life [back then] was not great."

To me, it seemed incredibly unfair that a woman who had

suffered so much as a child would have to suffer so much as an adult. Nobody deserves to have cancer, of course, but as my Aunt Tootsie once put it, "Betty couldn't seem to catch a break."

Betty's father, John Carey, supervised road-construction projects throughout Arizona and New Mexico. John, along with his wife Villa Claude. Betty and her little brother Jim lived in tent encampments for the construction crews and their families. Betty always thought her family was rich because their tent had a wooden floor, not just dirt.

11.
THE IMPOSSIBILITY OF COLLEGE

The lace ribbon had tatted edges, a dead giveaway that Junior had asked his mother to wrap his Christmas present for me. It was a little box, the kind one would use for, say, a diamond engagement ring.

We had agreed to exchange Christmas presents after going out for dinner at a "nice" sit-down restaurant, probably Pizza Hut. Likewise, I had Junior's Christmas present with me, something I had been saving up my money to buy. My present to him was also nicely wrapped. (It should have been, after all those hours spent in the wrapping room at Mom's store.)

"You go first," Junior said, putting the little box in my hands.

I untied the ribbon and peeled off the wrapping paper. It was a little hinged, velvet box. I opened it up and inside was a beautiful diamond solitaire pendant on a delicate gold chain. He clasped it around my neck. "It's nothing short of perfect," I said.

The necklace *was* perfect. While I thought it might have been an engagement ring, I was relieved that it wasn't. Junior and I had agreed that we were too young—and too broke—to get married right then.

Still, after opening such a sweet, tender-hearted gift, I knew that when he opened the present from me, the romantic moment would be lost forever.

"My turn?" he asked.

It would have been ridiculous for me to say that his gift wasn't ready or that there had been a mix-up of some sort. The present was in plain sight, wedged next to my thigh in our restaurant booth. The box wasn't huge, but it was unusually heavy for its size. So, I clumsily passed it across the table to Junior, then nervously watched as he tore the paper off. He pulled off the lid and parted the tissue paper on top. I waited for his reaction.

"Work boots," he said. But the tone of his voice betrayed no emotion.

"Not just work boots," I interjected. "They're steel-toed work boots."

I repeated the words, dragging them out for emphasis, "Steeeeel tooooooooed."

I was sitting on my side of the booth with a diamond necklace winking in the lamp light. Meanwhile, he was holding bulky footwear that was roughly the weight of a lead anvil.

"I have always wanted a pair of these! Thank you," he gushed.

At that moment, I realized two things. First, that Junior was just as pleased with his work boots as I was with my necklace. And second, he was kind enough to say "Thank you," when I had not.

"Thank you, thank you, thank you," I said, hoping to make up for being a knucklehead.

Days later back at our house on Hartup Street, Christmas Day was subdued. Mom's illness and the grind of the holiday sales season had taken a toll on all of us. But it didn't matter. We were well past the age of erector sets and Easy Bake Ovens from Santa Claus. There was one present, however, that brought joy to all of us.

My father handed my mother a plain manila envelope. She opened it and inside was an owner's manual for an automatic garage-door lift. He had installed it on the bay door where her store's freight was delivered. Never again would she or anyone else have to hoist the heavy door with a chain and pulley.

It was one of the most thoughtful gifts he had ever given her. Coincidentally, I had been thinking about that space too. There was a section just beyond the bay door that was used for storage. It measured roughly 40- by 30-feet and was full of mostly broken-down display racks, office chairs, and other discarded fixtures. The space did have one thing in its favor: plumbing.

I would be graduating from high school in the spring. If we cleaned out that storage area in the back of the store and added a bathroom and a kitchenette, it would make a perfect apartment for me. I could live at the store and work full time for my mother, at least until she was free and clear of cancer.

Her chemotherapy and radiation treatments were finished, but the residual effects went far beyond mere hair loss and would take months of recovery.

The fatigue was still almost debilitating, and most nights Mom went straight to bed after closing time. Her immune system was greatly weakened, so even a minor cold could turn into pneumonia. Because of chronic anemia, walking and long stints on her feet caused dizziness. Finally, her oncologist had prescribed several medications designed to reduce the odds of a recurrence of cancer, but these had their own side effects.

In general terms, cancer patients are considered "in remission" after five years and "cured" after 10 years.

Here was my plan: graduate from high school. Work and live at Mom's store for five years until she was in remission, then go to college. Then, Junior and I would get married. The downside: asking Junior to wait at least nine years, which was expecting a lot.

Here was Mom's plan: Bethy graduates from high school and goes directly to college.

"If you don't go to college now, you'll never go," Mom told me.

"That's not true," I said. "I will go when circumstances change."

"If by 'circumstances' you mean money, we will find a way to pay for college," my mother replied.

I wasn't referring to money, actually, but my mother was right. Even with federal or state grants, my tuition was going to be a challenge. The financial landscape in the world of hardware was changing.

Two companies, Lowe's and The Home Depot, were almost unknown in Kansas in the late 1970s. But not anymore. Both companies were undergoing rapid expansion, and these big-box retailers were putting small, independent hardware stores out of business. Some customers who used to go to B&G Hardware or Copeland Supply were now driving to Wichita to shop at The Home Depot.

To make my Mom happy, I applied at the University of Kansas, since tuition at a state school would be the most affordable option for a four-year college.

Soon after, there was a small glimmer of hope. One day, Aunt Tootsie was reading the classified ads in the *Houston Chronicle*. There, among the various job postings and apartment listings was a notice in 8-point type: "If you worked for one of Sid Richardson's oil companies, or if you are the descendant of someone who did, you may be eligible for a college scholarship from the Sid Richardson Memorial Fund." It included a mailing address for more details.

My aunt clipped out the ad and mailed it to my father. He, in turn, showed it to me. And with Dad's help, I replied to the ad:

I am the daughter of Homer Eugene Copeland, who worked for Mr. Richardson from February 20, 1948, until August 21, 1950, first at the Sid Richardson Carbon Co. in Odessa, followed by the Sid Richardson Gasoline Plant in Kermit.

I am inquiring about an application for a Sid Richardson Memorial Fund college scholarship. Please contact me using this address and/or phone number if you have questions.

Very sincerely yours,
Elizabeth Ann Copeland

Two weeks later, I received a reply:

Thank you for your inquiry. I have checked with the personnel office of the Bass/Richardson Companies. They did find a Homer Eugene Copeland whose employment date was February 20, 1948. However, the record ended there. We can only assume he did not work long enough to establish a record. The rules of the Fund require that a person be employed at least one year in order that his dependent may qualify. If you can find any proof that your father was employed for at least one year, then we would be able to provide an application.

I am so sorry that we cannot provide assistance at this time.

It was a setback, for sure, but I wasn't in a hurry to go to college right then anyway. Things were more peaceful at home than at any other time in my life. Ricky was happy and living with the same girlfriend. As far as my folks knew, his drinking was under control. Karan was living on her own and still working as a convenience store cashier. We rarely saw either one of them. Ronnie had graduated from business school and was working for a major tech firm in Dallas.

That's me at B&G Hardware during my senior year in high school.

In short, home life was blissful. As Mom got stronger, we sometimes had dinner on the back patio or played UNO in the evening. I experimented making Chinese food: My chow mein got a thumbs up. Not so for the egg foo young, which set up like a fruitcake. Junior came over and we helped Dad with his garden.

At school, I was heavily involved in the debate team, which traveled all over the state to compete against other teams in tournaments. I also entered various speech competitions held by civic organizations. I didn't win very many trophies, but I enjoyed learning how to research topics and think critically. I even mentioned to Mom that I could see myself becoming a lawyer someday.

That offhand remark must have planted a seed in my mother's brain.

One of Mom's regular customers was also her attorney, Bill. He helped my mother with things like contracts, real estate matters, and even her will. Bill came to the store for some project he was working on, and my mother waited on him. As Bill checked out at the front counter, she mentioned to him that I had expressed interest in becoming a lawyer. But she added that I was also considering staying in McPherson after high school, and maybe even getting married to Junior.

I can't say with any certainty, but I have long wondered whether my mother and Bill hatched some sort of plan. A few days later, Bill called me with a job offer as an after-school office helper at his law firm.

Working for Bill had many advantages. First, he paid better wages than my parents did. Second, he had a full-time secretary, Carol, who was wicked smart. Between Bill and Carol, I learned a lot about how the legal system worked. A third advantage, albeit a minor one, was that Bill had a little refrigerator that was fully stocked with free pop.

I mainly helped Carol manage Bill's appointments and phone calls. And there was a steady stream of paperwork that needed to be filed in clients' manila folders every day. Because of school, church, and the stores, I knew a lot of families in McPherson. Working in the law office exposed me to a different side of their lives. I knew when somebody in McPherson was buying property or being sued or even getting a divorce. But Bill made it very clear that all of that information stayed in the office and was never discussed publicly or even at home with my parents.

One of Bill's regular clients was very well known to me. His manila folder was one of the thicker ones in the filing cabinet because he had given Bill a lot of business over the years. That client was Ricky, my brother.

One day I came to the law office and, after helping myself to a Diet Coke, was filing various documents into the manila folders. About midway through the stack of paperwork, I came to a halt.

"Wait, this one pertains to Ricky," I said to Carol.

"Yes, I know," she said.

My brother had been charged with driving under the influence of alcohol a few days before, and Bill had accompanied him to court for the arraignment.

In the filing, the judge set a trial date, but no other details were given. But from Bill's notes, I saw that the officer who pulled my brother's car over registered his blood-alcohol level at 0.11, meaning he was severely impaired.

"Were my parents in court too?" I asked Carol.

"I don't know," she said. "You'll have to ask Bill."

When I turned toward his office, Bill was already standing in the doorway. He must have overheard our conversation.

"Were my parents in court too?" I asked him.

"No. Your parents don't know about the DUI," he said. "And since Rick is my client, they won't know about the charges unless *he* tells them himself."

Stunned, I went back to filing documents and answered a few phone calls until the firm closed. I was subdued at home that evening. I couldn't reveal Ricky's DUI to my parents, nor could I confront my brother about it. This was none of my business.

I was quiet for the next few days, but my folks didn't notice. They were busy getting ready for a visit from Larry, the son my mother bore when she was 16 years old. He was now 35 and lived in Arizona with his wife Alane and their children. Larry worked in a copper mine, and he and Alane owned a movie-rental business as well.

Larry and his family visited every two or three years. They had been putting off a trip to Kansas for almost a year until Mom felt stronger. But finally, it was clear that she had more stamina, seldom got sick, and was gaining weight. Her hair, which previously was black and straight, was coming in gray and wavy. Overall, her oncologist was pleased with her progress.

Larry and my mom had remained close over the years. She visited him in Arizona a couple of times, and they talked occasionally on the phone. At night, after everyone went to bed, Mom and Larry sat at the dining room table, smoked cigarettes, and talked.

On the third night of Larry's visit, everyone was in bed except for him and Mom. The phone rang, startling them both. My mother answered, but Larry could only hear one side of the conversation. Still, he knew that the matter was urgent.

"That was a nurse in the ER," Mom said after hanging up. "She told me to come quick to the hospital. Ricky has been badly beaten, and he is asking for me."

Mom, Dad, and Larry rushed to the hospital. The nurse said they were able to ID Ricky from the info in his wallet, and they knew to call the family because he scrawled "mom" on a piece of paper.

Mom and Dad found Ricky on a gurney waiting to have X-rays taken. His face was so badly beaten, he was practically unrecognizable. It was almost impossible to understand him when he spoke.

The X-rays revealed broken bones and lacerations to his face that would require plastic surgery to repair. The next day, Mom asked me to collect the most recent photos of Ricky so the plastic surgeon could use them as a reference.

Ricky was in the hospital for two days after undergoing the procedure. When he was released, he came home heavily bandaged for a long recovery.

"Why did he have to come back here?" I asked. "Can't his girlfriend take care of him at his own house?"

"It appears that Tracy left him a few months ago," Mom said. "He has been skipping work and is behind on his rent. There's no choice. His landlord threw him out, so he has to come home."

The next day, I went to school, but my mind was on Bill at the law firm.

When I got to the office, I found him at his desk.

"I have a question, but I know that ethically, you probably can't answer it," I said.

"Okay," Bill said tentatively.

"Is my brother an alcoholic?"

After a long pause, Bill said, "Yes, I believe he is."

Once Ricky was able to talk, we learned what had happened. He was at a bar downtown and got in a dispute with another man. My brother wouldn't say what it was about, but later we learned that the other guy was a drug dealer from Salina. The man found out where Ricky lived, broke into his mobile home, and beat him savagely with a baseball bat. After the man left, Ricky staggered to a few nearby houses to ask someone to call an ambulance. Finally, someone answered the door and called 9-1-1.

A few weeks into Ricky's recovery, my brother had his court appearance for the DUI, which Mom and Dad learned about for the first time. Ricky's license was suspended, and he was put on probation. He also had to attend alcohol rehab counseling.

What had been a blissful home life was now fraught with tension. Ricky's friends were coming to the house to see him, and with them came a certain lowlife vibe. I was certain he was still drinking, because he was erratic and surly.

To escape, I found myself spending more time with Junior and his family at their farm, where things were far more peaceful. *If we get married, maybe Junior and I can live at the farm until we get a place of our own,* I thought to myself. But I knew that would be the wrong reason to get married.

While this was going on, I received a letter in the mail with a postmark from Lawrence.

"Congratulations," it read. "You have been accepted to the Class of 1987 at the University of Kansas."

At the dinner table that night, I showed the letter to my parents.

"See," my mother said, "I knew you'd get in."

"Mom, they have to take me," I replied. "It's a Kansas state school and I'm a Kansas state student. And even though I've been accepted, we've still got to pay for it somehow."

"Who knows, that may be easier than you think," my father said cryptically.

I also called Ronnie in Dallas to tell him the news about KU. In fact, he's the one who helped me with the application, probably because KU was his alma mater. More than anyone else in my life, Ronnie had shown me that I had choices. When I was younger, I was a smart-mouth and could be a troublemaker, like Ricky. But Ronnie encouraged me to apply my brainpower to do something useful. That summer at Dad's store when he was the bookkeeper and I was his helper—really stuck with me.

The only person left to tell was Junior, but I didn't want to upset him. Increasingly, I was feeling like I wanted to go to college, but I was still concerned about how my family would cover the costs. Mom's health had improved, but relying on her to help with the tuition would be risky if she had a recurrence. I still had the option of waiting five years to save up some money.

"I got into KU," I told Junior the next day.

"Uh-huh," he said.

"I'm starting to think more about what it would be like to go to college," I admitted. "But that doesn't mean I'll go there right away," I added.

"True, but it's hard for one person to do a two-person job," he said.

The point he was making was that running a farm—or at least for his family—was a husband and wife effort. George and Barbara worked as a team to get the crops planted and harvested. George did the field work, but Barbara made sure everything else ran smoothly so he could focus on farming.

Graduation was just a few months away, and my future was still up in the air. That's when another letter arrived in the mail:

In response to your request, we are pleased to enclose an application form for an educational grant from the Sid Richardson Memorial Fund.

I had given up on getting a college scholarship, assuming that Dad couldn't prove that he had been employed at the oil company for at least one year. But in the attic, Dad kept a box with every single pay stub he had received from Sid Richardson from 1948 through 1950. Once again, Dad proved that he had the heart of a junk dealer. Nothing is ever thrown away.

He also called his former boss, Smokey Billue—who was still living in McPherson and just as irascible as he was in the dusty, windswept oilfields of West Texas. Whatever disagreements they may have had, Billue was happy to help my father. He wrote a letter certifying my father's employment dates. Billue's letter and photocopies of the pay stubs were mailed to the scholarship coordinator. With proof of employment, I qualified for the scholarship.

I was awarded a full scholarship to the University of Kansas that covered my tuition, my textbooks and other required materials, my room and board, and two round-trips home per semester. Money was no longer an issue.

I could go to college without burdening my family with this expense, and without having to work a job on the side to help cover my costs. I felt grateful and blessed and excited to see what the world looked like outside of McPherson.

I enrolled at KU, indicating that my interest was in journalism. I thought a J-school undergrad degree would serve me well in law school, not knowing yet that journalism was my true calling.

High school graduation came with the usual pomp and circumstance. Ronnie came home for the ceremony, and he gave me a tripod for the Nikon camera that my parents had given me as a graduation present. My mother had a little reception at our house after the ceremony, with punch and homemade cookies. Among the guests was Bill, the lawyer, who gave me a small crystal bud vase—which I still have today.

I also still have the pen and pencil set given to me by my friend and wingman emeritus, Arthur. I was going to miss him terribly. He had never married or had children, and his other family members lived out of state. Arthur seemed so alone to me. Other than drinking coffee at the store, his only social contact was at Mr. B's restaurant, where he ate practically every meal.

I had a short amount of time to gather everything I wanted to take to school—sheets, bedspread, towels, and the like. My mother recommended a small appliance called a "hot pot" that could be used to heat up soup. Since she had them in stock, I got one with my "daughter discount," meaning it was free.

Junior knew that I was busy getting ready for college, so there wasn't much time for us to see each other. He and his dad were busy with harvest, so neither of them would be back in the steel shop until the fall. Junior and I didn't break up, exactly. I just drifted away.

I had known George the Welder ever since I was a little girl when he worked at the junkyard. He helped my dad when he fell from the ladder, and he and Junior helped my mom when she had cancer. The two years that I spent with Junior and his family on their lovely farm were—and still are—among the fondest of my life.

In truth, I don't think I had the nerve—or the heart—to end our relationship kindly, which Junior deserved. And my callowness is something I regret today.

The day before I was set to leave for college, I stopped in at Mom and Dad's stores to say goodbye to the longtime employees and the coffee drinkers in the peanut gallery. They were very much my family too. Arthur brought in two dozen doughnuts, and I was surprised when I looked over and saw him and a couple of others with tears in their eyes.

"Okay, who gave you guys brain transplants?" I asked, with tears in my eyes too.

On my last evening in McPherson, I walked to Lakeside Park for some time to myself. As I circled the lake, I passed people picnicking, feeding the geese, and sitting on the banks of the lake with fishing rods. I think this walk was my way of saying goodbye to the little town that had nurtured me.

The following morning, I got up and loaded my car. I wanted to be packed up so I could say my goodbyes before Mom and Dad left the house to open the stores. They sat at the dining room table with me while I pushed around my Cheerios with a spoon.

"Well, we knew this day was coming," was all Dad said.

I couldn't speak, and Mom said very little. Instead, she sat at her post at the end of the supper table, smoking a cigarette. Standing on the threshold of a new, exciting college career, I should have been ecstatic, but I felt miserable.

"I should probably take off—I need to get my dorm room assignment," I mumbled. I don't know why I said that. Lawrence was only three hours away by car, and check-in at the dorm lasted all day long. But I just couldn't bear to sit there anymore.

My parents followed me out of the house and stood on the porch.

"If you decide you want to leave college and come home, then come home," my mother said as I got in the car.

It was about the nicest, most reassuring thing she could have said. I was always welcome back.

When I pulled up to my dormitory, Ellsworth Hall, it looked like a skyscraper to me. Then it struck me: the population of just this one dormitory was three times larger than my high school graduating class. The parking lot was abuzz with other students and their parents hauling in boxes and lamps and mini fridges.

Why didn't I think of a mini-fridge? I wondered.

I looked nothing like the beautiful sorority girls I had seen in the talent show that Ronnie took me to. I was wearing blue jeans with the pant legs rolled into a sloppy cuff, and a plaid, yoked shirt with mother-of-pearl snaps. In short, I looked like a bumpkin.

I parked in front of the dorm and brought in my first load. When I opened the door, my roommate was putting school supplies away in one of the desks. We introduced ourselves—her name was Lori—and discovered that we were remarkably alike. Both Kansas kids from small towns, and perhaps a little overwhelmed by how big Lawrence seemed in comparison.

When I went back to the parking lot for my next load, I saw a tow truck pulling away with my car hooked up to the back of it. I chased after the truck and hollered for it to stop, which probably looked pretty uncool to the other students. But the driver must have heard me, and he pulled to the side and stopped. For $20, he agreed to unhook my car. That $20 taught me my first lesson: Don't leave your car at the curb in front of the dormitory.

This time, I found a parking spot, and I filled my arms with my remaining things. When I got to my room, I took hold of the doorknob, and it was locked. I knocked, but Lori was no longer inside. I went to the main desk at the dorm to say I was locked out of my room. That's when I learned my second lesson: When you pulled your door shut behind you, it locked automatically. So, you had to carry a room key on you whenever you went out. In McPherson, we never locked our doors, even when we went out of town.

The first few weeks were rough. Homesickness hit me in waves that left me weepy and overwhelmed. To comfort myself, I clung to Mom's parting words: "If you decide you want to leave college and come home, then come home."

Months later, my mother shared with me that she had been struggling too. Each evening when she got home from the store, she turned on the radio to my favorite rock station out of Wichita. With the music playing in the background, she rationalized, it would at least *seem* like I was home.

In time, I adjusted to my new life in Lawrence. It was close enough to McPherson that I could go home if I wanted to, but far away enough so that I felt independent. I discovered that I fit in at college better than I ever did in high school. There were other students who were just as uncool as I was.

But just to be sure I would never forget the comforts of home, my mother occasionally sent a care package to my dormitory, and it was usually addressed to "Bethy Copeland." Inside were all sorts of homemade cookies, brownies, M&Ms, and other sweet treats—catnip for college students. Somehow my friends down the hall knew when a box arrived, and they would casually stop by my room to say "hi." There was plenty of food for everyone—Mom always made enough cookies for a crowd.

As she had told me many times before, "First and foremost, 'God is love,' but 'Food is love' is a close second."

12.
TIPPING POINT

"When I found him, he was unconscious," Dad told me later over the phone.

"Where was he?" I asked.

"About two blocks north of Frank's, just lying against the curb," he said. "I told his buddy to drive back to Frank's and call an ambulance."

Ricky had just left the bar on his bicycle. With a suspended license, his transportation was limited to just two wheels. That didn't stop him from drinking and driving, even if it was just on a bike. A couple of friends who were leaving the bar around the same time saw Ricky wipe out and hit his head on the curb. One of them drove to Mom and Dad's house and brought Dad to the scene.

The ambulance took Ricky to the hospital, where a brain scan indicated a fracture and some hemorrhaging. Nurses started an IV with drugs to reduce brain swelling and manage his blood pressure. His head wound had to be stitched up and dressed.

The ER doctor told the staff to start the admissions process, but Ricky—who was conscious at this point—insisted that he was perfectly fine. Dad persuaded him to stay just as a precaution.

Attendants wheeled him upstairs to a room and slid him into a bed. A nurse hooked him up to a monitor that measured his vital signs. By this time, it was 2 a.m.

At 6 a.m., Ricky was gone. If he was going to get better, he would do it his own way. It would be over a year before we heard from him again.

13.
REUNIONS

Dammit, dammit, dammit, dammit, dammit, I thought.

I was back in Lawrence, working on a story for the *University Daily Kansan* one afternoon when my newsroom phone rang. It was Mom. At this point I was a junior at KU, working for the student newspaper and doing some freelance writing for extra money on the side. Clearly, my mother had the good sense to call the newsroom because my irregular schedule meant I was never in my apartment. What Mom had to say brought everything to a halt.

"The cancer is back," she said. "I'm having more surgery, with chemotherapy and radiation to follow."

At my apartment that night, I had time to think things through. I couldn't be with Mom for the surgery, but with the semester coming to a close, I knew I could skip the following semester to be with her for the treatments. So, I applied and was accepted for a spring internship at *The Hutchinson News*, the same town where her cancer facility was located.

The managing editor there knew I was interning there for the sole purpose of taking my mother to her treatments. So, he made sure that my schedule was clear for several hours every Friday afternoon. For this I am eternally grateful.

I would pick Mom up at her store in McPherson and drive her to Hutchinson for lunch, then to the clinic for her treatment. After a couple of weeks of this, however, she couldn't bear to eat before her treatment, so we skipped lunch and drove straight to the clinic. It was pleasant and agonizing at the same time.

Mom continued to work at the store through all of this. One day around closing time, one of her regular customers came into her store to buy some wood screws. My mother was sitting in her office, and when she stood up from her desk, she found that she was unable to move her legs to walk.

"Warren," she called out from the office. "I'm tied up right now. Just go ahead and count out the wood screws you need and leave the money by the cash register."

After the customer left, Mom phoned my dad to come over and take her home. At the doctor's office the next day, she learned that the cancer had spread throughout her bones.

My mother had no choice but to liquidate her inventory and close the store. B&G Hardware's last day was a painful one for me. She started the business when I was in the second grade, and helping out there taught me so much about how things work. But more important, I was saying goodbye to the place where so many of my childhood memories took place.

The most precious gift to me was the time I got to spend with my mother, who was so amazing. On her last day in business, I sent Mom a dozen roses with a card that read, "Roses are red, tree bark is brown. The store may be gone, but the nut's still around!"

One small comfort was that her antique display cases were donated to a nearby museum in hopes that curators would someday recreate an "olde thyme" hardware store for visitors to experience.

After the store closed and Mom's treatments ended, I went back to college. For the next few years, my mother mainly stayed at home, holding court from her usual chair at the end of the supper table. Her friends and even some of her old customers came by the house to drop off food, jigsaw puzzles, and cheesy romance novels. And because she was such a good listener, they always stuck around to chat a bit.

Tootsie came up from Huntsville, Texas, to visit, and she and Mom sat at the table and smoked while my aunt told stories about her job at the courthouse. There she was known for inflicting informal straw polls on her co-workers, lobbing out seemingly random questions and tallying the votes. Among her poll questions:

"Do you get dressed from the bottom up, or the top down?"

"Do you think pastors are shorter than the national average of other professionals?"

"Do you brush your teeth after you get up, or after you eat breakfast?

Perhaps working in the county clerk's office predisposed Tootsie to collect data on anyone and everyone around her. In fact, those who fell into Tootsie's favor might be asked for the full names and birth dates of their mother and father. Weeks or months later, my aunt, an avid genealogist, would unfurl a detailed diagram of their family tree.

Tootsie also stayed busy playing bridge, and she had scads of friends. Visiting Mom was just another way to keep from getting lonely. Years before, Tootsie's husband Bobby had collapsed at an estate auction and died of a massive heart attack. His unexpected death at age 51 was a shock to all of us—the entire Copeland clan was incredibly fond of him.

My sister Karan's life had taken a traditional turn, which came as a surprise to all of us. She had fallen in love, gotten married, and became pregnant, but not in that exact order. Her infant, whom she named Alexander, came home from the hospital with my mom because Karan experienced some complications during childbirth. Alex cried and cried and cried, and nobody in the house could get any sleep. I suggested to Mom that she put her prosthetic breast inside the crib with Alex so he could suckle himself.

"Ha-ha. Very funny," she said.

Later, Karan struggled with both her moods and her marriage, so she frequently brought Alex to grandma and grandpa's house. While Alex played, Karan and Mom could smoke and chat a little.

Even Ricky came around. Mom and Dad knew that he was still in McPherson, but they only saw him in passing. As it turns out, my brother had been working hard to rebuild his life.

"After I left the hospital, I crashed at a friend's house," Ricky told Mom as she sat at the end of the table. "But a couple of months later, that guy kicked me out. So went to another buddy's house. He makes a living cleaning out rental houses and hauling junk to the dump. He let me sleep on his sofa on one condition—I had to help him with his hauling jobs."

"Can you even handle it?" Mom asked. "You banged your head pretty hard."

"At first I struggled," Ricky said. "I got dizzy, and the rotten smells at the dump made me sick to my stomach. I was always on the verge of puking. Maybe it was a good thing—I couldn't get near alcohol because just the thought of it made me queasy.

"When I got stronger, though, I got the itch to start drinking again. But my buddy tried to talk me out of it. Turns out, he was already involved in an AA group, trying to get sober himself."

"Did you go to 12-step meetings with him?" Mom asked.

"Nah," Ricky said with the wave of his hand. "I can't deal with all the boo-hoo stories everyone tells. And I'm not into the 'higher power' stuff, either."

"So, you're still drinking," Mom said with a sigh.

"No, no," Ricky said. "That's actually why I came by."

Ricky reached into his pocket and handed a bronze-colored token to my mother.

"They give this out at AA. It marks one year of sobriety," Ricky said proudly.

"But I thought you weren't going to meetings," Mom said.

"I'm not," he said. "My buddy goes to his meetings and has a sponsor. Then at home he walks me through the steps and acts as my sponsor."

"So where did you get the token?" Mom asked.

"He's almost a year ahead of me. So, I got his six-month token, and later he gave me this one-year token."

After graduating from college, I got a job on the news desk at a newspaper in Corpus Christi, Texas. That's where I met Chuck, a reporter on the sports desk. A native of Pennsylvania, Chuck had short, strawberry-blond hair and was the picture of physical fitness. That, combined with an impish smile and innumerable freckles, gave Chuck a certain look that said: "NASA astronaut."

My parents didn't hold back the when I brought Chuck home to Kansas one weekend to meet them for the first time. Before the visit, my mother had asked about Chuck's favorite desserts and was told "chocolate cake with white icing and banana cream pie." She made both desserts and said when he arrived, "I expect both of these to be gone by the end of the weekend, or my feelings will be hurt."

My father introduced himself to Chuck as a proud Democrat and an even prouder Texan, going as far to show my boyfriend the enormous, framed print of Sam Houston hanging under glass in the bedroom. Chuck mentioned that he had visited the famed Alamo recently while on a reporting assignment in San Antonio.

"REMEMBER THE ALAMO!" my father cried. He then took it upon himself to educate my Yankee boyfriend. "Hands down, the greatest battle in all of American history," he continued, clearly overlooking the likes of Bunker Hill and Gettysburg. "The blood that was shed there is what made this country great."

"Wait, I'm confused," Chuck said. "Didn't the Texans *lose* the Alamo and all of those inside the fort basically died?"

As my father seethed, I ran into the kitchen.

"Who wants more banana cream pie?" I called out.

Later that evening, Chuck was making small talk with my father, who was sipping his signature cocktail, a salty dog in a mayonnaise jar.

"I know that Beth is your youngest," Chuck said. "Did you always know that you wanted to have four children?"

"Oh, yes," my father said. "I once read that one out of every four people in the world is Chinese. So, I thought we'd better stop at four so I wouldn't risk having to learn a new language."

After working two years in Corpus Christi, I got a job on the copy desk at *Newsday*, a newspaper in New York. Chuck agreed to quit his job in sports and move with me to Long Island. The house we rented was located in a predominantly Italian hamlet near my workplace, and the landlord gave us a break because of Chuck's Italian surname. When we moved in, I weeded out the nerdy clothes from Chuck's closet, confident that he would thank me later. (He did not.)

Ronnie visited McPherson when he could. If Mom felt up to it, the two of them would go out for lunch. But by now, the cancer had honeycombed her bones, making walking precarious. And at this point she was on oxygen. So, Ronnie typically brought light meals and snacks to the house. On this trip, however, he brought something else: a girlfriend.

It surprised our family that Ronnie was even dating. First, he was very busy with his new job at a bank. But mainly, he was still very introverted and had trouble approaching women. He can thank his hairstylist for the breakthrough.

Ronnie went to the same man every month for a haircut. And every month, this stylist told my brother about one of his clients, who was also single and shared the same interests: baseball, travel, music, and the outdoors.

"I'm going to tell her about you, because you two would be great together," the stylist told my brother.

Every month, the woman client came to get her hair cut, and the stylist told her about Ronnie. Unfortunately, this woman was just as introverted as Ronnie, and she wouldn't let the hairstylist give Ronnie her phone number.

But the hairstylist persisted. He knew in his heart that his clients were a perfect match.

After several months, the woman, whose name is Nancy Jo, relented and gave the stylist permission to pass along her number.

The hairstylist gave the number to Ronnie, and true to form, he waited awhile before calling Nancy Jo. But finally, they went out. And on their first date, Ronnie knew in his heart that the hairstylist was right: They were a perfect match.

When Ronnie took Nancy Jo home to McPherson, the whole family knew it was a serious relationship. Bringing someone home to Mom was a first for him.

Mom was sitting at the end of the table, but she no longer smoked cigarettes because of the oxygen. Nancy Jo sat next to Ronnie at the table, but she clammed up. Mom told me later that she thought Nancy Jo was just nervous, but we realized later it's because Nancy Jo actually says very little in new situations.

Mom told me she liked Nancy Jo the moment she met her. And when Nancy Jo finally opened her mouth and said something, Mom said to her, "Bless your little pea-pickin' heart."

Nancy Jo was so touched, she began to cry.

A few months later, when Mom's condition worsened, I took a leave of absence from the newspaper to return to Kansas for a month or so. There, Dad and I lined up hospice care and equipped the house in a way that Mom could die at home—the place she loved so much. Hospice brought a woman named Gertie into our lives. She was such a blessing to our family because she went to great lengths to keep my mother comfortable.

Before my mother slipped away, my father wanted to find her brother Jim, the little boy who was in the car with her on the day their mother died in the flood. Mom and Jim had lost touch over the years, and nobody was sure where he was living. Dad called his sister Tootsie to enlist her help. She was still working at the courthouse in Huntsville and had ready access to public records. Maybe she could figure out where Jim was currently living, Dad thought. Tootsie zeroed in on New Mexico and Arizona, combing records county-by-county in both states. The search took about two weeks, but it yielded no clues as to Jim's whereabouts. Then, on a whim, Tootsie decided to search the records in Texas.

"I found him," Tootsie called Dad to say.

"Oh, my God, that's great. Where is he?" my father asked.

"Corpus Christi, Texas," she revealed.

It was the same city where I had first lived after college. What were the odds that my uncle and I had been living in the same place and didn't know it?

My father called Jim in Corpus Christi and explained that Mom's life was coming to an end. The next day, Jim embarked on a 12-hour drive to see his sister one last time. When he arrived at the house, my father ushered Jim into her bedroom. My mom recognized her brother immediately, Dad told me later, and they were able to chat a bit. Jim told her he was living in Corpus, but his job—he was involved in construction and mining—took him all over the world. He and my mother reminisced a bit, and they both actually laughed when Jim said, "Our grandfather. Boy, he sure was mean."

It was a joy that Jim looked happy and healthy—and that he and Mom could have closure on what had been very difficult childhoods for them both,

Shortly after Jim's visit, Tootsie wanted to say her goodbyes. But first, she needed to ask my mother a question. My aunt drove to McPherson and, like Jim, was ushered into the bedroom. She entered the room and found my mother weak but awake, lying in a hospital bed borrowed from the American Legion.

That's when Tootsie asked: "Betty, before I married Bobby, you said you had a secret about him. But you would only reveal it if I decided not to marry him. But since I did marry Bobby, I never learned the secret. Today I ask you, what was the secret?"

My mother's eyes were open and her heart was pumping, but little did my aunt know that Mom's mind had already crossed over to the other side. Fixing her gaze on Tootsie, my mother enigmatically whispered, "Moses."

Tootsie would never know the answer. Whether it was dementia or the fog of medication, my mother's mind was too far gone to understand the question and respond with a coherent answer.

Not long after that, Gertie told my father that Mom's days were coming to an end. She told her supervisors that she would be staying at our house "for as long as Betty needs me."

Dad moved a camping cot into the bedroom where Mom's hospital bed had been set up so he could relieve Gertie, allowing her to get some sleep.

Back in New York, I was in the newsroom one day in 1994 when my father called. "You had better come home if you want to say goodbye to Mom," he said.

The following morning, Chuck and I flew into Wichita, where a friend was waiting to drive us to McPherson. Ronnie, Ricky, Karan, and Larry had also been told that Mom's death was near, but they hadn't arrived yet.

Mom was unresponsive and her breathing was shallow when Chuck and I entered her room. Dad and Gertie were there at her side.

Looking strung out and exhausted, Dad said to me, "Since you're here to sit with Mom, I'm going into the other bedroom to get some rest."

Then Gertie had a request. "Today is my birthday, and my son wants to take me out for supper," she said. "If it's okay with you, I'm going to go out, but I'll come back if you need me."

After Gertie left to meet her son, Chuck reminded me that he and I hadn't eaten a thing that day. But I wasn't at all hungry. So, Chuck said to me, "You stay here. I'm going to walk to Wendy's and get something to eat. I'll be back in a bit."

It was just me and Mom in the room, and the only noise was the hum of an oxygen machine in the background. I didn't know whether she could hear me, but I took her hand anyway to say goodbye.

"I'm here now, Mom," I said. "Daddy is sleeping, and Gertie is out to supper with her son. Chuck came with me, and he is walking to Wendy's to grab a bite to eat.

"So, it's just you and me here right now. And I want you to know that Jesus is calling you home. And it's okay to let go."

I took a seat next to the bed and picked up the *McPherson Sentinel* on the table next to me. I had been reading the newspaper for just a few minutes when Mom's breathing changed. It had a sort of rasp to it.

"Take a deep breath, Mom," I said.

The rasping continued, and I returned to her bedside. "Take a deep breath, Mom," I said a second time.

Then she exhaled.

It had been 12 years since Mom's initial diagnosis of breast cancer. After a helluva fight, she succumbed to the disease at 62 years old. But Mom's fight didn't begin 12 years ago. It began the moment the floodwaters swept her mother's car into the canyon.

Betty Copeland had survived trauma and neglect and abuse as a little girl. She was treated poorly by the man she married when she was just 16 years old. She wed again in hopes of creating a better life for herself, but that too failed. After each setback, she kept on going, finding jobs, and eking out a livelihood single handedly.

Meeting my father marked a turning point in her life, one for the better. "He saved me," she once told me.

Later, with a young family, Mom could see that money was going to be tight with only one breadwinner. So, she told my father that she wanted to buy the hardware store and run it herself. Over the 15 years that her store was open, my mother built a profitable business and made lasting friendships while doing so. I was so incredibly proud of her. Standing by her bed as she took her last breath, I was relieved that she could finally rest.

The day after Mom died, my father and I were going through

her pocketbook so we could remove her driver's license and credit cards. That's when we found a slit in the lining. My father reached inside and pulled out a $100 bill that had been hidden there. The money was accompanied by a hand-written note from my mother: "Eugene, you'll need to go buy coffee and cups for after the funeral."

Mom had a beautiful funeral service, and the church was overflowing with plants and flowers—just like when she "secretly" went into the hospital all those years ago. So many well-wishers attended that the police department had to stop traffic as the hearse carrying her coffin and scores of cars behind it could make their way to McPherson Cemetery.

When I got back to New York after the funeral, I resumed my life at the newspaper on Long Island. I was grieving, but I was happy to know that my mother's suffering was over. Still, whenever I went to a restaurant and saw what looked like a mother and daughter laughing and enjoying their lunch, waves of jealousy would wash over me.

For a long time after her death, I often wondered why my mother waited so long to ask a physician to examine her breast, which by then was visibly deformed. I also wondered whether the outcome would have been different had Mom gone to Kansas City or another major medical center for treatment instead of staying close to home.

Since then, I have let it go. I feel blessed by the countless ways that she enriched me as a person. And I'm so incredibly grateful for the 29 years that I had her in my life.

Mom's death made me think harder about the relationships in my life, mainly Chuck. We had been living together for four years—an arrangement that had deeply troubled my parents.

"When are you going to make an honest man out of him?" my father once asked.

I didn't know what to reply because Chuck was about the most honest person I had ever met.

Within a few months of my mother's death, Chuck and I started talking more seriously about marriage. We had pushed off these discussions in the past, in part because Mom had been so ill. But now, the time felt right for both of us. We didn't want a fancy wedding with prime rib, a Champagne fountain, and a live band. Doing the chicken dance in front of 200 guests wasn't exactly a lifelong dream for either of us.

We didn't even have a guest registry, which probably would have disappointed my mother, because helping couples make their selections was one of her favorite duties at the store. But somehow my father must have known that we needed hardware in our lives, and it came in the form of a wedding present.

"Beth, come out front and help me carry this," Chuck hollered from our driveway one day.

A UPS truck was pulling away from our house in Brightwaters, New York, leaving Chuck standing next to an enormous box that was bursting at the seams. It weighed 150 pounds—so unwieldy, in fact, that we had to borrow the neighbor kid's skateboard to move it from the driveway into the house.

I recognized my father's handwriting on the address label and wondered if he was sending me a bunch of cast-iron tools from his collection. That would be highly unlikely—those artifacts were too precious for him to give away. Chuck slit the box open and inside was a large metal cabinet containing four sliding metal drawers. Each drawer was divided into 24 individual compartments with a printed label on each one. Every type of fastener imaginable was in there, along with all sorts of other handy things—liquid graphite, worm-gear clamps, corks, cotter pins, toggle bolts, fuses, cup hooks, faucet washers, axle caps, and more.

On the side was another label: B&C Hardware. Chuck and I were getting married.

14.
THE SUMMER OF 1995

If I had a zillion dollars, I would buy a perfume factory. Inside there would be a long conveyor belt carrying hundreds of bottles. The belt would line up the tops of the bottles under little spigots that would fill them up with a new, second fragrance that my factory would make. Its scent—worn by men and women alike—would evoke feelings that occur only in adulthood, and hopefully on only one day in a lifetime. I would call my fragrance: Wedding Day.

I would wear my bottle on a chain that hangs around my neck. And whenever I'm having a bad day, I would take out the stopper and breathe deeply. My lungs would fill with the scent of fresh cut roses and a whiff of cologne. The aroma of breath mints and lip balm hang in the air. I would let the feelings of unbounded joy and unlimited potential wash over me. I imagine myself—

"...to light the unity candle," the pastor said.

—in a house with my new husband and a cat named Daisy. We're lounging on the patio, where a fountain is set among the climbing roses—

"Um, Beth? Please join Chuck at the altar, and together you will light the unity candle," the pastor said a second time.

After we lit the candle that signified our bond, I turned and looked out over the pews. The ancient, cavernous church was mostly empty. In all, there were 10 of us, including the pastor, in attendance on our wedding day.

My dad took his place at the pulpit to recite the scripture that Chuck and I had chosen. Opening the Bible to the first chapter of the Book of Ruth, my father began to read:

Wherever you go, I will go. Wherever you live, I will live. Your people will be my people, and your God will be my God. Wherever you die, I will die, and there I will be buried. May the Lord punish me severely if I allow anything but death to separate us.

I was 30 years old on my wedding day, and my mother had been dead for roughly a year. Chuck and I cried a little as we faced each other in front of the altar. But assuredly, they were good tears.

My brother Ronnie came from Dallas with his new wife Nancy Jo. Four of our closest friends were also there.

Then we traveled to Western Pennsylvania to celebrate with Chuck's friends and family in the little town of New Wilmington. There, about 75 people joined us under a tent on the rolling lawns of Chuck's aunt's house. The highlight was a table literally covered with homemade cookies—a beloved tradition in this part of the state. The turnout consisted mainly of Chuck's uncles, aunts, and cousins on both his mother's Polish side and his father's Italian side. My husband's parents had both died young, and he was an only child. But the Poles and the Italians on both sides gladly treated him like a brother and a son.

Our next stop was McPherson, where punch and cake were served in the reception room at the Baptist church. Among the guests were Bob and Lois—our dear family friends with the fried-chicken restaurant. They gave me an antique bottle from a local doctor's office that had long been closed. This artifact became the latest addition to my collection, the one started by Junior's mother when we dug for bottles during the harvest. Junior had since gotten married to a woman who came to McPherson for college, and together they had two children. Arthur, my wingman from Dad's store came, too, mainly because he wanted to ensure that the groom met his standards. As a wedding present, Arthur gave us a clay trivet imprinted with two heads of wheat.

Ricky didn't come, but he gave me a gift, a canister set with giant sunflowers, the Kansas state flower. He was still single, still a hell-raiser, and still sober. I know now that alcoholism is a disease, and Ricky worked hard to beat it. He is my hero, just like when we were little kids.

My brother lived in a trailer park in a little town north of Wichita, a risky choice of abode considering it was in Tornado Alley. But since his mobile home had a sort of carport-type structure built over it, "tornadoes wouldn't recognize it as a trailer when passing over," he rationalized.

Meanwhile, my father was adapting to his new life as a widower. It started with my mother's $100,000 life insurance policy, which Dad dutifully used to pay off his store building. Having that paid off eased the day-to-day pressure of running his store.

Given a choice, my father would have likely sold his house on Hartup Street and lived alone in his little apartment in the attic of Copeland Supply. But he was largely responsible for Alex, Karan's son. Living with my parents had given Alex some stability in his life, since we had a better understanding of what Karan was dealing with, bi-polar disorder. It, too, is a disease, one that has no cure. My sister works hard to manage it with medication, nutrition, and by controlling her environment. It takes a heroic effort on her part, and I have so much respect for how she copes.

In truth, Alex was as good for my dad as Dad was for him. My father helped him with his homework and school projects, and Alex helped my father restore the old tools that had been pulled out of the junk decades before. They traveled to a number of places—including one trip to see me in New York.

Travel had always been something my father enjoyed. About a month after my mother's funeral, Dad drove all the way back to Gallup, New Mexico, and he stayed at the El Rancho, the place where he had first met my mother. Dad had been so stoic about my mother's death, but this trip to New Mexico showed me just how much he was hurting.

One person, however, was able to cushion the blow: Gertie,

my mother's hospice caregiver. Our family asked if she would be willing to give up her apartment and come to live at Dad's house as a sort of housekeeper. My father was 69 at the time and still busy with Copeland Supply. Having someone to oversee the household would be ideal, but mainly, he needed help taking care of Alex.

Happily, Gertie agreed to stay on. We fixed up the back of our house so that Gertie could have a private bedroom, a bathroom, and a sitting room to herself. The new arrangement was a blessing to both of them.

My father ran Copeland Supply for almost a decade after my mother's death. At one point, he gave me the option to buy him out and take over his store. But I had the good sense to say no. I had made a life for myself as a journalist, and Chuck ran a small business of his own in New York. I loved McPherson, but I knew I couldn't come back.

When Dad turned 75, he got an offer that was too good to refuse, and he sold his business. He called me to give me the news.

"Bethy, it's time to piss on the fire and call the dogs," he said, using an old hunting expression.

On his last day of business, he threw himself a big party, complete with beer and snacks. The event lasted all day, and included a visit from the mayor of McPherson, who presented Dad with a congratulatory proclamation from the city.

"Can I keep the frame?" Dad asked. Like I said, the heart of a junk dealer.

To commemorate Dad's last day, I made bumper stickers that were handed out to all of the customers (except the teetotaling Baptists) who came into the store. The stickers read, in part, "I got hammered at Copeland Supply."

At some point during the day, my dad walked over to the ice chest to grab himself another beer.

"Dad, don't you think one beer is enough?" I asked him.

Then, he used another one of his favorite lines. Popping the can open, Dad quipped, "Bethy, a bird can't fly on just one wing!"

Even though his store was gone, I still put Dad to work. His phone invariably rang whenever Chuck and I undertook a DYI project at our house in New York, a 1933 Tudor that needed a lot of TLC. Putting up crown molding, painting the basement floor, rehanging a sticky door—he gave us step-by-step instructions for all of them.

Most all of them, anyway.

Once Chuck and I were hanging a new light fixture over our dining room table. We turned the power off and removed the old fixture. Coming out of the hole in the ceiling were six wires— where we had expected to see just three. The brittle wires were all black, making it difficult to discern the "live" and neutral wires, as well as the wire for the wall switch. I called my dad and explained the situation.

"Can I turn the power back on and use a circuit tester to figure out which wires are live?" I asked.

"No, because it doesn't address the problem—you have a lot of old wiring inside of an old house," he said.

"Do you know what I should do to fix that?" I asked.

"I know exactly what you need to do," he said. "You need to hang up the phone with me, pick it up again, and call a professional electrician. You have no business messing around with electricity."

Clearly, with age comes wisdom. And Dad had the wisdom to tell me I was in over my head—literally.

With proceeds from the sale of Copeland Supply, Dad built himself a large, metal warehouse-style building on a piece of land that he kept back when he sold the junkyard. There he opened The Pioneer Heritage Museum and displayed his massive collection of cast iron tools, pulleys, hay hooks, and other relics of frontier life.

Most impressive was his wall of wrenches—hundreds of them in a variety of quirky shapes. Many of them were designed to repair farm implements, and a single wrench could have as many as nine different functions, such as a hammer, a pry bar, and multiple wrench heads in different sizes. The ledge around the perimeter of the museum was lined with cast iron tractor seats, and just looking at them made my butt hurt.

One summer my dad threw himself a big party to celebrate turning 100. About 30 of his closest friends showed up for a cookout to celebrate the milestone. People brought "You're 100!" birthday cards and wore pointy party hats. And of course, there was a chocolate sheet cake with "100" on the top. Ricky provided the entertainment in the form of an air gun he made that shot baking potatoes high in the sky.

The thing is, Dad was only 78 at the time.

During a pause in the festivities, somebody asked my father, "Cope, why are you having a 100th birthday party if you're only 78?"

My father had his answer ready: "I want to celebrate turning 100 while my friends are still alive, and Bethy doesn't have to wipe the drool off my mouth."

At 78, Dad threw himself a 100th birthday party so he could enjoy the celebration while his friends were still alive. Behind him are some of the antique tools in his vast collection.

In time, maintaining the museum got to be too much for my father. In his 80s, he decided to auction off the antique wrenches—along with hundreds of other artifacts of early frontier life. He signed a contract with an auction house that advertised the sale to antiques collectors across the country. There was a great turnout, with heated bidding. In a surprise to him, all of those antiques became sort of a 401(k)-retirement fund for him. Under his stewardship, the antiques had appreciated over time, and he chose the right time to sell.

In truth, I never thought he would part with those relics, certain that he instead would figure out a way to weld them to his casket. But it made him happy knowing that other collectors would cherish the antiques as much as he did.

After the sale, Dad spent his days at a ramshackle hangout where you could glimpse slivers of daylight through the wallboards. The drinking water from the tap was sketchy, so he brought jugs of water from the house on Hartup Street. And skunks lived underneath the building. I begged him to hang a sign on the door that read: "My Daughter Does Not Want Me to Be Here."

After Copeland Supply closed, Dad decamped to a ramshackle barn,
where he drank coffee and ate peanuts with the same
retirees who hung out at his store all those years.

But he was content. Most important, Dad was never lonely. Why? Because he brought along two "fixtures" that had been with him from the very beginning: the coffee pot and the peanut warmer. Every morning, Arthur and his band of coffee-drinking retirees showed up at my dad's new hangout to shoot the breeze and solve the problems of the world.

And to talk about hardware.

REFERENCES

[1] *"Oil Embargo, 1973-74"* (U.S. State Department Office of the Historian, undated).

[2] Michael Bryan, *"The Great Inflation, 1965-1982"* (Federal Reserve Bank of Atlanta, undated).

[3] John M. Berry, *"Prime Rate Is Raised to a Record 21%"* (The Washington Post, Dec. 17, 1980).

[4] Vince Peterson, *"Effects of 1980 Grain Embargo Echo Through the Years"* (U.S. Wheat Associates, April 14, 2020).

[5] *"Managing the Crisis: The FDIC and RTC Experience"* (Federal Deposit Insurance Corp., June 12, 2023, p. 46).

[6] Neil Harl, *"Farm Debt Crisis of the 1980s"* (Wiley-Blackwell, 1991)

[7] Michael A. Urquhart and Marillyn A. Hewson, *"Unemployment continued to rise in 1982 as recession deepened"* (Bureau of Labor Statistics Monthly Labor Review, February 1983, p. 9)

[8] Garfinkel L, Boring CC, Heath CW Jr. "Changing trends. An overview of breast cancer incidence and mortality" (Cancer, July 1, 1994, p. 74)

ACKNOWLEDGMENTS

Growing up, few kids my age knew the difference between a hack saw and a back saw. But I did. For this, I can thank my parents. They also showed me that hardship is no barrier to success. That girls can fix things just as well as boys. That mistakes can be forgiven. That women make great "businessmen." They made me feel loved, especially when I didn't love myself so much. My older siblings, Larry Brickey, Ron Copeland, Rick Copeland, and Karan Rumple all cared for me and nurtured me in their own way. My aunt, Eleanor Browder, and uncle, Jim Carey and his wife, Barbara, were instrumental in helping me piece together the timeline and in filling in some narrative gaps. And when I think of these people even now, a burning ember deep within my heart pulses and glows.

Had this story unfolded anywhere else in the world but McPherson, it wouldn't have been as special. So, I'm thanking my hometown and the good people past and present who have made it great. McPherson has always punched above its weight, especially in an era that saw jobs lost to overseas manufacturing and retail sales shift to big-box stores and the internet.

I can't overlook Chuck DeCarbo, my husband of 30 years, who has heard the stories within the pages of this book too many times to count. When I meet someone new, he knows to search out a comfortable chair. His lips subtly move along with mine as I recite the same old stories to my captive listener. His patience has no end, and I thank him for that. (And for putting up with my family.)

This book exists because of Larry Rout, my *Wall Street Journal* editor. He featured the story of my parents' side-by-side stores on the front page of the Journal's Small Business section in May 2024. The article generated hundreds of comments and emails, and with Larry's encouragement, I set out to write this memoir. After an early setback, when my publishing prospects dimmed, Larry prodded me to keep going.

Larry is good at prodding. Swamped with copy, stuck in meetings, or pressed on a deadline, Larry still finds time to sharpen my ideas and turn my drafts into polished copy. After my story runs, he lets me take all the credit for how great it turned out. As if.

And on the rare occasion when I'm not my best self, Larry lets me moan and mewl a bit. Then we talk about movies.

I am proud to be among the stable of writers at Topeka, Kansas-based Flint Hills Publishing. Company president Thea Rademacher is not only a bad-ass publisher, she also champions the rights of authors and the need to protect their copyrights. Also at Flint Hills, my manuscript was deftly edited by Nathan Fredrickson, who made sure that my story was heartfelt and true, but not, to quote a Broadway show tune, "as corny as Kansas in August."

Book Club
Discussion Guide

1. The narrative focuses on the author's experience at her parents' hardware store. What are some of the themes covered in this coming-of-age account?

2. Think about some of your favorite shops. What are some of the elements and traits that make you want to come back? Did Copeland Supply and B&G Hardware share any of these traits?

3. How old were you when you got your first job? What are some of the lessons it taught you?

4. Many people say they're yearning for "simpler times." What does that phrase mean to you?

5. With Betty and Gene so involved in their stores and communities, do you feel like their children and home life suffered?

6. What are some of the life lessons that your parents taught you?

7. Bethy was very emotional when she left home for college. Was it difficult when you moved out of your family's home for good?

8. The book gives a number of examples where the church and community stepped up when the family was in crisis. Are there similar examples–where friends and neighbors pitched in— when you or your family were going through a difficult time?

9. Could you see yourself living in a place like McPherson? On a farm? Or would you prefer a larger city with a faster pace of life?

10. What message do you wish your grown-up self could have given to your little-kid self to make things less scary or painful?

ABOUT THE AUTHOR

Beth DeCarbo is a lifelong journalist who most recently covered real estate for *The Wall Street Journal*. Previously she was the deputy business editor at *Newsday* on Long Island, N.Y., and the features editor at *The Atlanta Journal-Constitution*.

She grew up in a small farm town in Kansas working for her parents, who owned competing hardware stores next door to each other on Main Street. At 18, she left home to earn a journalism degree at the University of Kansas. Today she lives in the mountains of western South Carolina with her husband, Chuck, their dog, Biscuit, and two cats, Jam and Butters.

At heart, she is a storyteller who likes to shed light on the human condition. In their spare time, she and her husband fearlessly tackle home improvement projects, a few of which turn out halfway decent.

To learn more about Beth, go to her website at www.CopyTK.com. For more background and insights on hardware and independent retailers, visit Beth's blog at bethdecarbo.substack.com.